**WARNING!**

This book is not for the weak of heart. Pregnant women, those with injuries to the brain or spine, and people shorter than fifty-eight of these books stacked on top of each other should think carefully before perusing these pages. They contain tips, spoilers, horror stories, bizarre facts, and other insider information that will thrill you, chill you, and give you an unfair advantage over your friends and rivals.

Even if you know the secrets, amusement park games are difficult to win. This is particularly true if you do not practice or pay close attention. Don't come running to us if you lose your whole paycheck on a fixed game like Three Cats.

The stunts in this book *should never be attempted by amateurs*, particularly those mentioned in the "Freaks and Geeks" section. Sword swallowing, fire breathing, and Human Blockhead take years of practice. Even dull objects, if shoved far enough down your esophagus or up your nose, can cause major damage. You are all amateurs, so do not try these tricks at home.

# CARNIVAL UNDERCOVER

by
Bret Witter

Illustrations by
Lorelei Sharkey

A PLUME BOOK

PLUME

Published by the Penguin Group
Penguin Putnam Inc., 375 Hudson Street, New York, New York 10014, U.S.A.
Penguin Books Ltd, 80 Strand, London WC2R 0RL, England
Penguin Books Australia Ltd, 250 Camberwell Road, Camberwell, Victoria 3124, Australia
Penguin Books Canada Ltd, 10 Alcorn Avenue, Toronto, Ontario, Canada M4V 3B2
Penguin Books (N.Z.) Ltd, Cnr Rosedale and Airborne Roads, Albany, Auckland 1310, New Zealand

Penguin Books Ltd, Registered Offices: Harmondsworth, Middlesex, England

First published by Plume, a member of Penguin Group (USA) Inc.

A LifeTime Media Production
LifeTime Media, Inc.
352 Seventh Avenue, 15th Floor
New York, NY 10001

First Printing, May 2003
10 9 8 7 6 5 4 3 2 1

Copyright © LifeTime Media, 2003
All rights reserved

 REGISTERED TRADEMARK—MARCA REGISTRADA

CIP data is available.
ISBN 0-452-28428-7

Printed in the United States of America
Set in Serifa Roman, Blast-O-Rama Bold, Journal Ultra.
Designed by Amy V. Wilson

This book is dedicated to
Elizabeth Butler, for personal reasons,
to Kelly Notaras, for professional reasons,
and to all the carnies,
for every other reason imaginable.

**Carnival:** A cooperative business arrangement between independent showmen, ride owners, and concessionaires to present outdoor entertainment for the public.

**Fair:** An exhibition, as of farm products or manufactured goods, usually accompanied by various entertainments; an event, usually for the benefit of a charity or public institution, including entertainment and sale of goods.

**Amusement Park:** A commercial enterprise that offers rides, games, shows, souvenirs, unreadable maps, questionable food, long lines, public drunkenness, and other forms of entertainment, usually for about 50 bucks plus parking.

# TABLE OF CONTENTS

## 4 Thrills, Chills, and Kills: Carnival Rides Revealed

| Key to chapter symbols you'll see throughout this book |  | Carnival Confidential: Top Secret Insider Information |
| |  | *Score!: Tips to Improve Your Carnival Skills* |
| |  | Terrible but True: Tales of Disaster and Death |

# INTRODUCTION

If you want to know the secret, don't ask a carny. But give me two dollars [the price of a round], and I'll give you a quick lesson in how this game is played.

—Unnamed Carny, Columbia County Fair Shoot the Star booth

If there's one thing I've learned while researching and writing this book, it's not "Don't ask a carny." Many carnies are nice, helpful, and surprisingly normal people, as long as you keep plunking down dollars and don't ask too much about their personal lives. Most carnies will hesitate to tell you their name (although "Ask Red or John down at the Speed Pitch" was a commonly heard piece of advice), and they certainly aren't going to tell you how to beat the game, but they're perfectly happy to tell you a few quick truisms about the carny life.

No, what I've learned is that there are a whole heck of a lot of fairs, carnivals, and amusement parks in this country. Just about every town with a stoplight has a fairground, and the good people of Anywhere, U.S.A. love to throw a party when the fair's in town. You could make a whole summer out of visiting carnivals—I mean every day of the entire summer—and never leave your home state. From Rhinebeck, New York, to Ames, Iowa, and from Puyallup, Washington, to Plant City, Florida, there's a world of wonder just waiting to be discovered on the other side of the parking lot.

I'm not ashamed to say that my love affair with the fair began at the North Alabama State Fair (notice how regional fairs are often called "state" fairs) in about 1978. I remember walking right in the gate and stopping dead in my tracks. There, inside a glass cube on a 5-foot riser, sat a man with an enormous beard. This beard wasn't made of hair, though, it was made of thousands of crawling, buzzing bees. How could a red-blooded American kid not get hooked?

This book isn't just about fairs. That just wouldn't be . . . fair, now, would it? This book is about any place with a ride, a game booth, and a few food vendors, from honest-to-god amusement parks to boardwalks and sideshows. Is it about thrills? We've got everything you'll ever need to know about roller coasters and other wild rides. Is it about chills? There are enough disasters here to keep you up every night for a year. Is it about skills? I'll teach you how to humiliate your friends and walk away with the biggest stuffed animal (and the cutest girl) every time.

In the end, though, this book isn't about winning; it's about fun. And there is nothing more fun than summer outdoors in America. If you don't agree with that, you can put this book down and walk away right now. As they say in the carnival, your money's no good here.

Actually, they never say that about money in the carnival. That's the first of many lessons you're about to learn.

# 1

# Step Right Up, Ladies and Germs!
# The Carnival Experience Revealed

Who doesn't love a
carnival, fair, or
amusement park? They
have everything you
could ask for: Fried
food, dangerous-looking
rides, macho games, freak
shows, meat-on-a-stick,
champion milking cows, and
teenagers dressed up as giant
stuffed animals.

If that's not America, what is?

# Preparing the Devil's Sandbox

Amusement parks and carnivals are a devil's bargain. They exist to amuse, to thrill, to entertain, but also to manipulate. You are given pleasure; in return, you are separated from far more money than you ever planned to spend.

This is manipulation by design, from the towering rides you can see for miles down the highway to the ludicrously expensive hot dogs that are always just a few feet away.

Designing an amusement park or carnival is a science, albeit not quite on the level of rocket propulsion or organic chemistry. But like the real sciences, it does have rules for success. The first is location.

In the heyday of the amusement park (1910–1930), there were more than 2,000 parks in the United States. Most were family-owned and located in large urban areas or at the end of brand-new subway or trolley lines. The Great Depression hit the industry hard, and by the end of World War II less than 500 parks were still in business. The 1960s closed most of the remaining city parks, as customers moved to the suburbs.

In the 1970s, the amusement business went corporate, with owners like Paramount, Universal, Marriott, and Anheuser-Busch, the maker of Budweiser beer. These companies had a formula (just like a real science): parks must be near an interstate highway and within 50 miles of a major metropolitan area. The business of building parks boomed . . . for a decade. By 1980, all major markets in the United States were served by at least one large-scale amusement park. Only nine new parks have been built in North America since then; your money now goes to pumping up existing parks to mega-proportions.

Meanwhile, thousands of carnivals and fairs continue to serve every dot on the map, from street fairs in Manhattan to annual celebrations in the most rural counties in America. The size of the local population is no deterrent to the traveling showman, and he certainly doesn't need an interstate highway. The carny organizer is only looking for three things:

1. **Ample parking.** If there's not enough parking, customers won't come. There just aren't enough Americans willing to take the bus—unless the carnival is located in Atlantic City or Branson, Missouri, and aimed at retirees.

2. **Ground-based power source.** Ride operators won't go near power lines, since even carnies know it's unwise to swing metal near electrical wires. Carnivals always keep the wires on the ground.

3. **A flat, well-drained area.** Rides can only operate safely on relatively level ground, and no one wants a Ferris wheel to fall over. Meanwhile, if the lot doesn't drain well, it *will* rain, the grounds *will* flood, and the crew—or worse, that award-winning chicken—*will* be electrocuted by the previously mentioned exposed ground wires.

Fairgrounds are carnival locations of choice because they are designed with these three factors in mind. They are also well known enough to overcome the first unwritten rule of customer behavior: If it's remotely possible to get lost on the way to the carnival, a majority of people will.

# Interior Design

The classic carnival is built around a central walkway, known as the Midway. The Midway originated at the Chicago World's Fair in 1893, when the designers built a long artificial pond in the center of the fairgrounds and put all the major attractions alongside it. They crowned their "Middle Way" with the daddy of all carnival rides: The George Ferris Giant Wheel, which at 264 feet towered above the rest of the park. The Ferris wheel is still the central attraction on many Midways, although the low-speed, easygoing ride doesn't thrill the modern adrenaline junkie like it did those Victorian fogies.

In the classic layout, the Midway is surrounded by parallel aisles of goodies. Each type of attraction—rides, food, games, farm equipment, souvenirs, etc.—is grouped together in the hope that sheer repetition will dazzle poor rubes into plunking down their cash. How many corn dog stands can a human pass, after all, without falling prey to the temptation? And why stop at just one? There are four more carts in plain view claiming their corn dogs are the best. Don't you want to compare them all? And top them off with a delicious funnel cake?

If you're confronted with a Midway, the key to maintaining your fiscal sanity is to walk across the aisles, not down them. That way you get a variety of choices—food, game, ride, ride, game, food—as opposed to passing twenty rifle games in a row, which makes it impossible not to pick up a gun and shoot something.

The Midway, soon known as the Boardwalk when a beach was nearby, was the centerpiece of the American amusement park for more than sixty years. Then, in 1955, Disneyland changed everything. The stroke of genius? Disneyland was the

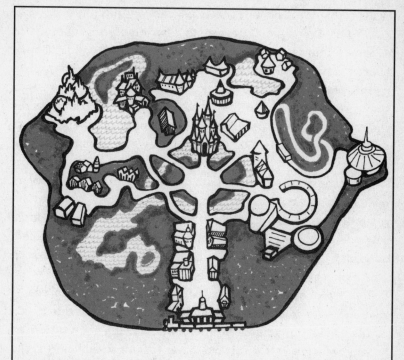

Disney's magic doughnut (with a sweet castle center)

first park designed to appeal to the emerging laziness of the typical postwar American. Midways and boardwalks are specifically designed for leisurely strolling, a proverbial taking of the air. Modern Americans don't want air; they want convenience.

The Midway is a grocery store, where you're expected to walk up and down the aisles sampling the wares. Disneyland is a wheel, designed to speed you to your destination. The park is a series of themed areas, connected in the center by a giant landmark: Sleeping Beauty Castle. It's a short walk from anywhere in the park to the castle; from there, it's a short walk

6

to any other location. Two short walks always make a short walk, right? Well, no, but this is psychology, not physics.

The Disneyland designers also created a number of "secret" routes that don't take you past the castle. These shortcuts not only decrease walking time even more, they make people think they've gotten hold of insider information, that they're somehow "working" the park. This is exactly what they're designed to do: Make people feel so good about their day, and their own intelligence, that they keep coming back for more.

Disneyland also broke another tradition of Midway design—it mixed up the food, the games, the souvenirs, and the rides. In fact, it morphed them into a sort of mega-attraction: The ride-a-souvenir-o-eatery-show. These days, even the toilets at Disney have a souvenir stand attached to them . . . although bathroom eateries have yet to catch on.

The idea behind the exit store-o-restaurant, of course, is that a stream of customers is forced to come off the ride or out of the show right past the merchandise. It's temptation by accommodation, but surely customers aren't so naive? Yes, the average human loves trinkets, but surely they can recognize a shameless manipulation designed solely to draw hard–earned money out of their pockets?

Which brings us to the second unwritten rule of customer behavior: Never, ever overestimate the customer. If it's possible to fall for it, fall they will.

# The Carnival Lot

At the amusement park, every man, woman, child, and animal (real, animatronic, or stuffed with a teenager) works for "the Man," but carnivals are an entirely different bird. Every booth and ride at the carnival is owned and operated by an independent contractor, so it's every man for himself.

Carnivals are run by booking agents. These agents select the location (called the lot), organize the layout, handle the permits, and pay for promotion. They make money by parceling the lot into sites, then renting the sites to independent contractors. A carnival generally lasts five to twelve days, and a standard 10 x 10 lot will run an operator anywhere from $50 to $150 a day, plus electricity and other expenses. The total can easily reach $1,000 a week, so if the carny isn't bringing down steady business, he's going broke.

Pricing varies from carnival to carnival based on the reputation of the location and the booking agent. But each lot in a carnival rents for the same price per square foot, despite the fact that all lots are not created equal. Naturally, the competition for the best lots is fierce. For a prime location, the "tip" (never called a bribe, of course) for the lot man, the person who assigns the sites, can run as high as 10 percent of gross proceeds.

- **The best site on the carnival lot is the first booth on the right, just inside the main entrance.** Most people naturally turn to their right, so the right side of the aisle is generally worth 5 to 10 percent more business than the same booth on the left side.

- **The second best site is near the entrance to the main stage**, where show "blow-off" can give you a flood of business. Since the main stage is usually near the carnival entrance, this is a double whammy of profit.

- **The third best site is on the Midway near one of the main attractions**, like the Ferris wheel or the roller coaster. These rides are hot spots, and their heat will usually trickle over to nearby booths.

While the formula seems easy, the logistics can be difficult, especially when you have to fight a hundred other operators at 10 a.m. after driving all night to reach the carnival site (not to mention the hangover). Good lots can turn into losers, called "blanks," by drawing a bad neighbor like the water slide (too muddy) or anything smelly (cow barn, trash collection point, Port-o-Let). Amateurs are often fooled into thinking they're getting a hot spot near an entrance, only to find out later the entrance is hardly ever used or closed during certain hours.

In general, as you move away from the primary entrance, the sites get less desirable. The back end of the Midway, away from the entrance, is low-flow, low-profit territory. Should it be avoided by savvy customers? Of course not. The game owners at the back of the lot are newbies, so they often have the easiest games to win. At the very least, they're less likely to fleece you out of $20 by talking a good rap.

Rent for a standard twelve–day carnival is usually collected on Wednesday night and the last night of the show. These are the best times to hit the back booths, because many operators will be desperate to "make their nut," the carny term for covering expenses. If you're ever going to get a deal, a desperate, inexperienced game owner trying to make a quick buck is going to be the one to give it to you.

The opposite logic applies to food carts. You want your foodies experienced and selling. The last thing you need is to plunk down green for food that's been sitting around all night, so hit the booths near the entrance—that's where the pros sling hash.

# Carny Psychology 101

There are people at carnivals, fairs, and amusement parks whose job it is to take your money. These people are called carnies. They will bait you; they will insult you; they will befriend you. It's nothing personal. The carny has only one goal, and it's always the same: To get you to spend your money.

To bait you, the carny must first spot you. That's why you should never wear bright colors, show your belly button, or gel your hair into a pompadour for the carnival. A nondescript outfit is known as "carny camouflage" because it helps you blend in with the crowd. If you aren't wearing it, you're tempting the carny to go for the throat. He will insult your manhood or womanhood; he will pick on your appearance; he will compliment your date a bit too sincerely.

Do not be suckered. Don't stop and ask him to repeat the last comment. Never challenge a carny. If you allow yourself to be drawn in, you will be parted from your money, and perhaps your dignity.

To paraphrase Bill Murray in *Groundhog Day*: Do not play carny games angry.

Don't misunderstand this message—carnies are not unfriendly. They are new in town, and they don't know anyone but the gang they rode in with, so they're often hungry for human interaction. Simply put, carnies are always looking for a buck and companionship, in that order. Often the companionship involves taking your buck, but that's life with a carny.

Carnies will compliment you. They will flirt with you and wink at you. They will give you a free ball if you miss your first toss. They will tell you the "secret" of the game you're playing. Don't be fooled—it's all part of the hustle.

# What are the signs that a carny's attentions are sincere?

**1** He crosses over from behind the counter and stands next to you.

**2** He lets you hold a prize.

**3** He gives you a prize to keep, which is practically a declaration of love. Prizes are carny currency, after all, and carny currency doesn't come cheap.

# Dressing Right

The name of the game in carnival wear is comfort. You're going to be walking several miles before the day is done, so think ahead and leave the stylish gear at home: It's only going to attract unwanted carny-attitude anyway.

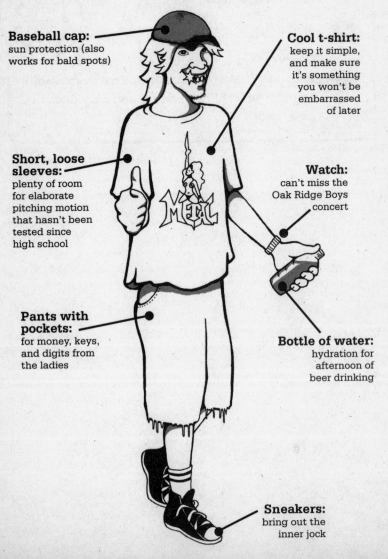

**Baseball cap:** sun protection (also works for bald spots)

**Cool t-shirt:** keep it simple, and make sure it's something you won't be embarrassed of later

**Short, loose sleeves:** plenty of room for elaborate pitching motion that hasn't been tested since high school

**Watch:** can't miss the Oak Ridge Boys concert

**Pants with pockets:** for money, keys, and digits from the ladies

**Bottle of water:** hydration for afternoon of beer drinking

**Sneakers:** bring out the inner jock

# Dressing Wrong

If you forget the name of the game (it's comfort), you can be in for a long day. This isn't the opera, after all. Unfortunately, there are at least nine ways to go wrong.

**Flask of vodka:** dehydration or embarrassment (or both) are imminent

**Big hair:** always a fashion faux pas

**Dangly earrings:** yes, they can get caught on the Zipper cage

**No sunscreen:** tomorrow you'll look like Lobster Girl

**Cut-off t-shirt:** carnies will be all over you like flies on roadkill

**Pregnancy:** uh-oh, stick to the kiddie rides

**Fashionable purse:** only carnies will be impressed with your daddy's money, and that's not a good thing

**Skirt:** if you're going to ride, wear pants— or at least nice panties

**High heels:** blisters aren't sexy or fun

# Sneaking In: Amusement Parks

Gate prices at large amusement park are, well, obscene. Walt Disney World costs you $50 for a single–day pass. Kennywood, the great roller–coaster park in Pennsylvania, costs $30. Season passes are a better deal—you can ride all summer at Magic Mountain for only $90—but that's still a pretty serious bite out of the wallet.

In other words, it's worth it to work for a discount. If you're under seventeen, ask for the kid's price. If you're over fifty, act like a geezer. Local products, businesses, and hotels often offer coupons, so take advantage of their generosity. If you don't live in the area, call ahead and find hot deals through the local Tourist Board. Parks don't care; they just want your business. Most parks offer discount information on their websites.

Of course, it's not exactly rebel behavior to pass a coupon to a gate attendant, which is why the cool kids are always sneaking in. In the good old days, even the best parks had all sorts of secret entrances, including a little-known path through the swamp near Walt Disney World's Space Mountain. Sorry Charlie, those innocent times are gone. It's all fences and razor wire now.

Unless you know a park really well, don't try to find a back path or scale a fence. Large parks have private security forces, and in these days of heightened alert some guards have guns . . . and itchy trigger fingers. If you try to sneak over (or under) a fence, remember: Bombs and weapons, even when fake, aren't funny. Don't give that rent-a-cop an excuse.

Besides, you're much more likely to nab a free day using your brain, not your feet. The simplest scam is to stand at the park entrance and try to bum a ticket from a large tourist group—or, even better, a company field trip—that may have overbought. If you look pathetic (or crazy) enough, someone may take pity on you. A small child is always a useful prop, but it is not acceptable to abandon the kid once a ticket is secured. (Fortunately, the really young ones can often be paid off with a quarter or a lollipop.)

Another option is to befriend a park employee. At Disney World, employees have their own key cards, entrances, and parties. Of course, this is a long-term strategy that necessitates either living in the area or spending a lot of vacation time hanging around trying to turn strangers into generous friends with party invitations to spare.

If you're adventurous, and you have a friend, try this classic scam:

Your friend buys a ticket and enters the park. Ten minutes later, he exits the park and gets his hand stamped for reentry. While the ink is still wet, you place your hand against his and transfer the stamp. The fake stamp will be a reverse of a real stamp, so smudge it up a bit. Remember to do all this out of sight of the gate. Otherwise, you're not just an idiot—you're busted.

Your friend should reenter first. That way he's safe. Wait five minutes and then try to "reenter" the park yourself. Don't act suspicious or criminal. Many parks are on to this scam, so you might get asked some uncomfortable questions. Don't panic. What's the worst that could happen?

On second thought, never mind. If you're going to break the law—and sneaking into an amusement park is a serious crime—then it's best not to think of the consequences.

# Worth the Risk?

People will do stupid things to save a buck. They'll get up at dawn, hike for miles, scale a barbed-wire fence, swim a moat . . . all to save that pesky park admission fee. Perhaps you've been working on such a plan yourself.

Is it really worth it? Yes, entrance fees are exorbitant, but are you going to enjoy a day spent stinking and wet from swimming that stagnant pond? Or a hot afternoon with a dozen cuts on your arm from that rusty old fence?

Thomas Cleveland apparently decided the reward was worth the risk when he scaled the 16-foot fence at Disneyland and climbed onto the monorail track. His plan was to walk along the track until he was inside the park, then jump down to freedom. Seems like the perfect way to save a few bills, right?

Except for the fact that where there are monorail tracks, there are monorail trains. Instead of jumping down into the arms of the waiting security guards when the train came into sight, Cleveland decided to climb down and lay on the support a few feet under the track. Unfortunately, there wasn't enough clearance. Cleveland was struck by the train and killed, and his mangled body was dragged for more than 40 feet.

Young, dead, and never even got to ride the Matterhorn: You can all learn a valuable lesson from Tom's tragic error in judgment.

Sneaking in? Sometimes it's just not worth the risk.

# Sneaking In: Fairs and Carnivals

Traveling fairs, carnivals, and small amusement parks work on a different economic model than the big daddies. Entrance is usually free (or reasonably priced), but once inside you pay per ride.

Outside of printing counterfeit tickets, there's no smart way to sneak onto a pay-per-ride. Some people try to run to an empty car after the operator closes the gate and begins inspecting the seat restraints. This never works. When it does, that's even worse: If the operator is inspecting straps, he has to lock you in place from the outside. If he doesn't know you're on, he's not locking you in. That, kids, is how accidents happen.

Besides, if the operator is that careless with the passengers, just think how careless he is with the maintenance. Everybody, even the paying customers, should stay off that ride.

**Walk the Walk.** The best way to save money at the carnival: Don't park in the pay lot. You can always save five bucks by parking elsewhere and walking ten minutes. Just remember where you parked: There's a good chance someone in your group is going to be bloated and/or drunk at the end of the day, so take note while you're all sober.

**The Gravy Train.** If there's a cover charge for entry, try to fake your way in. Watch what kind of people get a free pass, because impersonating them can punch your ticket. If Pepsi signs are all over the park, throw on a Pepsi cap and act like the local bottling center's assistant night supervisor. Sponsors have a long gravy train, and there's a good chance the guards will let you slide.

**Candid Camera.** Filming a fake documentary is golden, since people do the darndest things when there's a camera in their face. It doesn't take much more than a handheld video recorder, a "crew" of three close friends, a movie idea that sounds vaguely plausible (saying you're from *Playboy* will never work), and a clipboard with some fake production notes to pull off this stunt. But don't forget to interview the ticket taker!

**The Local Yokel.** Even better is to bring an item being judged at the fair, such as a home-baked pie or some extra–large onions, and act like you're in the competition. Most judging, especially of baked goods, takes place before the fair opens, so go ahead and get some blue ribbons at a local party store. If you're going to fake that you're in a competition, you might as well fake that you won it, right?

Remember, to make the "local yokel" work, you must know something about the item that is supposedly your pride and joy. If the guard asks, you not only need to know what kind of pie you've brought, but at least three steps in how it was baked. That's why veggies are easier: If you've got half a brain, you can always talk your way through a fake agricultural technique.

# Safety Standards?
# What Safety Standards?

These days, most people probably assume fairs, carnivals, and amusement parks are heavily regulated. That assumption is wrong. The federal government has absolutely no safety jurisdiction over fixed amusement park rides, such as those found at permanent parks like Walt Disney World or Six Flags.

Thirteen states don't inspect their amusement parks, or even have written regulations governing them. Only four of those thirteen states require a private inspection certificate or insurance card. That leaves nine states—almost 20 percent—with absolutely no safety mechanism in place for their fixed amusement parks.

The State of Florida does inspect amusement parks. However, the law allows the state only to inspect permanent facilities with fewer than 1,000 full-time employees. A state safety official admitted this was the result of political pressure from a few large amusement attractions in the state, who prefer to hire private inspectors.

California, meanwhile, had no safety inspections until 2000, when a hard-fought legal battle resulted in new amusement park regulations.

Mobile amusement rides, such as those found at traveling fairs and carnivals, are actually more closely regulated than fixed rides. They fall under the jurisdiction of the Consumer Products Safety Commission, which has the power to shut down the losers. In addition, all but eight states require yearly inspections, and all but six have regulations governing ride maintenance and operation.

Make you a little squeamish? Wondering if you live in a state with no safety inspections or requirements? Don't worry: Inspectors agree that on the whole, rides are extremely safe and well maintained. Said one California official: "There's so much competition for amusement dollars that the only way a carnival can compete is to become sophisticated. There's no real safety concern."

# Top 10 Amusement Parks

It's not about the number of visitors; it's the thrill of the action. Still, you've got to hand it to these parks for bringing in the warm bodies, even if the rest of the Top Ten are sucking Disney's fumes. As you can see, Disney's Magic Kingdom has more visitors than the nos. 3 to 6 parks combined, and that doesn't count Epcot Center, which draws more than 9 million visitors a year. No wonder it's the happiest place on earth—if you own a piece of the action.

| Park | Visitors |
|---|---|
| 1. Disney's Magic Kingdom, Lake Buena Vista, FL | 14.8 million |
| 2. Disneyland, Anaheim, CA | 12.35 million |
| 3. Busch Gardens, Tampa Bay, FL | 4.6 million |
| 4. Knott's Berry Farm, Buena Park, FL | 3.59 million |
| 5. Six Flags Great Adventure, Jackson, NJ | 3.56 million |
| 6. Morey's Pier, Wildwood, NJ | 3.4 million |
| 7. Santa Cruz Boardwalk, Santa Cruz, CA | 3.0 million |
| 8. Six Flags Over Texas, Arlington, TX | 3.0 million |
| 9. Six Flags Great America, Gurnee, IL | 2.9 million |
| 10. Six Flags World of Adventure, Aurora, OH | 2.75 million |

Based on 2001 actual attendance. Cultural centers, studio tours, and animal parks were not included on this list.

# Top 10 State & Local Fairs

When many people think of state fairs, they think of Iowa and its rabid crowds, top-notch entertainment, and giant cow sculpted from 600 pounds of butter—a fixture at every Iowa State Fair since 1959 (and recently copied by Utah, of all states). But with only 1,008,000 visitors in 2002, Iowa didn't even crack the Top 15 most popular fairs. Amazingly, these fairs last only about ten days before someone has to dismantle the whole darn thing.

| | |
|---|---|
| 1. State Fair of Texas, Dallas, TX | 3.0 million |
| 2. Minnesota State Fair, St. Paul, MN | 1.76 million |
| 3. Houston Livestock & Rodeo Show, Houston, TX | 1.38 million |
| 4. Western Washington Fair, Puyallup, WA | 1.2 million |
| 5. L.A. County Fair, Pomona, CA | 1.17 million |
| 6. Eastern States Exposition, West Springfield, MA | 1.13 million |
| 7. Illinois State Fair, Springfield, IL | 1.13 million |
| 8. Del Mar Fair, Del Mar, CA | 1.13 million |
| 9. Arizona State Fair, Phoenix, AZ | 1.08 million |
| 10. California State Fair, Sacramento, CA | 1.05 million |

Based on 2001 actual attendance.

# Fighting the Crowds

About 270 million visits are made to North American amusement parks, carnivals, and fairs each year. One out of every twenty of those visits is to one park: Disney World. That's 14.8 million visitors per year—or an average of 40,548 people per day.

Does that mean that an average day at Disney World is the most crowded amusement spot on earth? Hardly. Disney doesn't even come close to the average daily attendance of large state fairs.

Take the New York State Fair, which in 2002 attracted 1.02 million people. Sounds small compared to Disney World, right? Not so, since the New York State Fair lasts only twelve days. That means an average of 85,000 people went to the fair each day. That's twice the daily average for Disney World.

And the New York State Fair isn't even close to the most attended fair in the country. In fact, it's twelfth. The number one-ranked State Fair of Texas attracts a whopping 3 million visits every year.

Of course, Disney World doesn't attract the same number of visitors every day. Some days (like a rainy day in the middle of October) are leisurely strolls down an open Main Street; others are nightmares of obese, sweating rubes. If you want to avoid the crowds at Space Mountain, you have to remember a few simple rules:

- **Don't go to Disney three days to a week after a holiday.** People overthink their strategy, so the park is emptier on the holiday and the day after the holiday than it is a few days later.

- **Don't go to Disney in August.** The park is packed, and it's just too freaking hot.

- **Don't go to Disney for Spring Break.** This rule needs no explanation.

- **Don't go to Disney on the day of a special event** such as Graduation Day or Gay Pride Day unless you really, really want to attend that event.

If you want great coasters without all the animatronic hoopla, simply don't go to Disney.

# The Dirt on Disney

There are a lot of rumors about Disney World and Disneyland, and some might even be true. Here are a few of the most interesting and helpful, with a special thank-you to all the Disney lovers (and haters) who obsess over every detail.

**RUMOR: You can get discount tickets at those colorful booths that line the roadsides of Central Florida.**
**TRUE OR FALSE? False.** They're scams. By the time you realize the pass is bogus, that vendor and his booth are long gone.

**RUMOR: Walt Disney World Resort is roughly the size of Oshkosh, Wisconsin.**
**TRUE OR FALSE? False.** It's roughly the size of San Francisco. Not only is it huge, it's the largest single-site employer in the United States with more than 54,000 wage slaves (or as Disney calls them, "cast members").

**RUMOR: Disney kept long-haired males out of their parks until the late 1960s as part of an "unwritten" dress code.**
**TRUE OR FALSE? True.** Facial hair and halter–top restrictions have also been in place from time to time. In 2000, Disney finally did away with some of the hair restrictions for employees. Now male Disney employees can sport mustaches—neatly trimmed, of course. (Though why anyone would want to wear a mustache is another question.)

**RUMOR: There are tunnels under Disney World.**
**TRUE OR FALSE? True.** They're called utilidors (clever Walt-speak for utility corridors), and they can be visited by normals on a few unadvertised early morning tours offered through the Disney lodges. Just ask at the desk.

**RUMOR: There are no security cameras at Disney World.**
**TRUE OR FALSE? True.** No actual pictures are ever taken of guests at Disney. However, the Mouse has ways: The park uses infrared cameras to detect, well, everything.

**RUMOR: Disney World does funky stuff with the garbage.**
**TRUE OR FALSE? True.** Disney trash is sucked at about 60 miles an hour through a series of underground tubes to a central location every twenty minutes. If you're in the park and you could swear you just heard a tornado pass by, that was probably garbage hurtling beneath your feet.

**RUMOR: There's a secret lounge in Disneyland's New Orleans Square.**
**TRUE OR FALSE? True.** And it's a great place to get loaded if you're of age. It's located next to Blue Bayou, and marked by a brass plaque that says: 33. If you knock on the door and know the password (meaning you have a reservation or are a member), you will be whisked to an exclusive second-floor dining room in an antique–glass elevator. Dinner is expensive, about $80 per person, but Club 33 is the best place inside the park to catch the fireworks.

**RUMOR: There's a basketball court inside Disneyland's Matterhorn.**
**TRUE OR FALSE? True.** Unfortunately, it's for employees only.

**RUMOR: Nothing's free at Disney.**
**TRUE OR FALSE? False.** The Coca-Cola gift shop at Epcot's IceStation Cool features free Coke products from around the world, like delicious melon soda from China and the terribly bitter club soda-like Beverly from Italy. After fueling up and cooling down, sneak around to the exit behind the iceberg to avoid getting snowed in.

**RUMOR: There's a way to cut to the front of the line at Space Mountain.**
**TRUE OR FALSE? True.** The door to a VIP room with air-conditioning, refreshments, and access straight to the front of the line is off to the right of the main entrance. The catch? You have to be an employee of ride sponsor FedEx—or at least have a FedEx identification card. (Unaware that FedEx sponsored Space Mountain? You either haven't been to Disney recently, or you somehow missed all those people FedExing packages to Mars in the on-line video.)

**RUMOR: Every evening, when the lights come on at Space Mountain, the floor is covered with false teeth, toupees, and bras that have fallen off riders.**
**TRUE OR FALSE? False.** Unfortunately, bras don't just fall off.

**RUMOR: The best place to view the Fantasy in the Sky Fireworks Display is Main Street U.S.A.**
**TRUE OR FALSE? False.** To end your day the right way, take the monorail to the observation deck on the roof of the Contemporary Hotel. It's the perfect place to see the fireworks, and it's entirely free!

## 2

# Stuff Yourself Sick:
# Carnival Food Revealed

One of the chief pleasures of the carnival, and especially the fair, is the food. If it can be fried, dipped in chocolate, and/or served on a stick, it's here . . . for only two to three times the price you'll pay in the rest of the world. So go on—stuff yourself sick.

# Buying the Best

Not all carnival food is created equal. Some vendors care about quality, while others are slinging junk just to make a buck. The good news is you can easily tell the two apart. Since they don't have air-conditioning, carny carts are designed with large open sides to let in fresh air. Conveniently, this lets customers see what's happening inside. Always check out the action before you buy.

The most important thing to remember is that great carny food is fresh carny food. If a carny isn't making your order on the spot, or if you can't see where the food is being prepared, move on to the next booth. Unscrupulous carnies can and will buy precooked food and pass it off as cart-cooked. Don't be fooled. There's always something cooking elsewhere on the Midway, and you have the right to a carny corn dog that's fresh-dipped, not frozen.

Carny carts are inspected by local health officials, but that doesn't mean they can't be disease-ridden filth traps. Although no actual statistics are kept, it's a sure bet you're more likely to be hospitalized by carny food than by a carnival ride, so use common sense.

- **If the booth looks dirty or smells bad, don't buy.** That's food poisoning in your future.

- **Never buy from a booth that uses a microwave.** Real carny food isn't nuked. Bake ovens, hot oil fryers, and specialty equipment are signs of quality.

- **Avoid booths that sell more than seven items, not including drinks.** The food in these mega-booths often sits around for hours, if it's made there at all.

- **Never buy fish or chicken at a carnival.** Fish gets rank fast, especially in the sun. Chicken is a nasty visitor when undercooked. Both are far more likely to land you in the hospital than good old beef, pork, or meatlike substitute.

If you want good carny food every time, learn to identify the two types of vendors: Professionals and 40-milers. Forty-milers are vendors who travel only to nearby fairs or who rent a booth for just one event. They are often local groups like the 4-H Club, Rotary Club, or church organizations. You can usually spot 40-milers by their unsophisticated booths, which often employ handwritten signs or chalkboard menus. If you're unsure of an operator's status, just ask. There's no shame in being a 40-miler, so most will 'fess up.

If you want nonstandard carnival food like barbeque, vegetables, pie, or multiple-course meals, buy from 40-milers. If you want carnival classics like corn dogs or elephant ears, visit the professionals.

While carnival food is heaven-on-a-stick, amusement park food is awful and overpriced. If you're going to buy food, you have to buy it from the park, so why should they bother to make it good? The key here is to eat as little as possible. Plan ahead with a sizable breakfast, and realize you can always sate your hunger with a dinner at the Big Boy a few miles down the highway.

If you must eat inside, choose something simple and all-American, like a hamburger, hot dog, or nachos. Amusement park pizzas are expensive and almost universally disappointing. Salads are lame, but safe. The food bar next to your favorite roller coaster is not the place to try gourmet items like guacamole or poached fish for the first time. The bad experience could turn you off these tasty treats for life.

# The Carnival Food Pyramid

The carnival food pyramid was created by a supplier to coax customers (carnival booth operators) into carrying more products. It's useful here to show the level of depravity you are predetermined to sink into once you're past the carnival gate. Items do vary by region—barbeque in the South, black ice cream in Iowa, Tex-Mex in the Southwest—but the fact remains: You will be unable to resist eating at least four items at your local carnival and, unless you're a vegetarian, they will fall into these four categories.

**The base of the pyramid is the meats:** Hot dogs, corn dogs, sausage, pork-chop-on-a-stick, turkey legs, and all the other animal parts that form the centerpiece of a standard carnival meal.

**The second level is the salty snacks:** Popcorn, nachos, pretzels, and French fries. These are the perfect "sides" for that big slab of pork chop or Italian sausage. Even if the foods are eaten an hour apart, they're still just part of one continuous meal. Pizza combines these two levels—it's a main dish and a side in one— which is good for the customer but sucks for the vendor.

**The third level marks the move to desserts, which comprise two basic categories: Pastries**, such as elephant ears and funnel cakes, and **frozen treats**, such as lemonade, smoothies, ice cream, and sno-cones. This is the point where the average customer begins to become excessively full. However, there's one more irresistible level to go.

**Sweet snacks like sugary "kettle" popcorn, caramel apples, and cotton candy are the pinnacle of the carnival food pyramid.** Maybe you can only handle a bite, and maybe you succumb to nausea and vertigo soon after, but it's a rare customer who resists purchasing one of these carnival delights. The brain and stomach say no, but the heart always cries out for just one taste.

Not your USDA recommended diet

No one is saying the carnival diet is healthy, but is it enough to keep a human being alive for a sustained period of time? Numerous carnies have tested this boundary over the years, and the answer, 90 percent of the time anyway, is yes.

# Our Friend Sal(monella)

Outbreaks of food-related illness occur with startling frequency even in our fastidious world, and like hurricanes on the Gulf Coast or earthquakes in California people always act surprised. Meanwhile, roaches are everywhere; flies crawl all over your funnel cake while you're ogling a passing strumpet; you forget to wash your hands after tightly clutching the eighty-three-year-old safety bar on the Tilt-a-Whirl. It's not even worth thinking about what's fallen into that deep-fat fryer over the years.

Health issues do arise from time to time in the presence of food, even at fairs and carnivals. And yes, even at the crème de la crème of amusement parks: Disney.

In August 2001, Walt Disney World hosted the U.S. Transplant Games, a premier athletic competition for organ-transplant recipients. Unfortunately, an estimated 141 of the organ-transplant athletes went home sick and disoriented.

The cause was traced to a batch of pre-packaged diced Roma tomatoes served at six of the park's restaurants. The tomatoes had been infected with salmonella, a rod-shaped bacteria that causes health problems from headaches and fever to life-threatening infections. Those most likely to suffer serious complications are children, the elderly, and . . . organ-transplant recipients.

Though no one died in the Disney salmonella incident, let this moment stand as a testament to the awful truth: If food poisoning can happen at the "Happiest Place on Earth," it can happen anywhere.

# Cotton Candy

Cotton candy. The very phrase conjures an image of rickety rides, cheap games, strange odors, blaring disco, and flashing lights. Want a carnival on a stick for less than two dollars? You've got your wish with this fluffy, colorful candy cloud.

But what is this melt-in-your-mouth confection? Believe it or not, your average cone of cotton candy is nothing more than 1 ounce of crystallized sugar (about 7½ teaspoons) and one drop of food coloring. That's why it disappears so quickly on the tongue: It's mostly air. It's that air that makes the candy so . . . cottony, and it's the cotton that keeps the kiddies (and adults) coming back.

The "cottoning" process is ingenious in its simplicity. Heat is used to melt the sugar, which is then spun rapidly in a special machine. The spinning pushes the sticky sugar through tiny holes, stretching it into long, thin strands that are almost lighter than air. The operator twirls a cardboard cone across the holey surface in the opposite direction of the spinning strands, and the result is a beautiful cloud of candy, warm and ready to eat.

The sugar cottoning process was invented by William Morrison and John Wharton, candy makers from Nashville, Tennessee. The two entrepreneurs debuted their concoction in 1903 and hit the jackpot at the 1904 St. Louis World's Fair, where they sold 68,655 boxes of "Fairy Floss" at a quarter apiece. Their total take of $17,165.75 would be worth more than half a million dollars today. Everyone, of course, wanted a piece of the action. Within a year, cotton candy was available across the nation.

Early cotton candy had an added cachet: danger. The floss machines were loud, hot, and prone to spewing hardened sugar chunks. Even worse, the interior canisters were made of glass and would often chip during the high-speed spinning process,

The chimp-proof system

embedding small glass slivers in the candy. Painful to the unlucky floss eater, no doubt, but there are no records of fatalities.

The modern, danger-free cotton candy industry began in 1949, when the Gold Medal Fun Products Company (no, they're not the makers of the flour) bought the design for a metal, belt-driven, vibration-free floss machine from an Indiana carny. The machine was not only so safe and easy to use that a child could operate it (not recommended), but it added a new dimension to the lure of fairy floss: Gawkers could now stand around watching the carny spin his wares. And as all cotton candy lovers know, watching floss being made is half the fun.

The other half is eating it. The two go hand-in-hand because the best cotton candy is straight out of the floss machine. If you want the tastiest treat, make sure the candy is freshly made. Anything else is a sucker's buy.

Never, ever purchase bagged cotton candy, no matter how much the carny insists on its freshness. "Fresh," in carny speak, is anything less than two days old—and even five-minute-old cotton candy is not as good as the just-spun stuff. That bagged junk is strictly FDO: For Display Only.

Despite rumors to the contrary, color does affect taste. Blueberry, bubble gum, banana, and other flavors are all common at today's carnivals, although it often takes a sensitive palate to tell them apart.

Although artificial banana-flavored sugar would seem to have almost universal appeal, classic pink is still by far the most popular candy color. But two-colored cotton candy, which can now be spun fresh in one canister (ah, technology!), outsells single color cotton candy almost two to one, especially if one of the colors is pink.

While making cotton candy is so easy it can be spun by a blind chimpanzee (very not recommended), there is one catch: You gotta have the equipment. The process is simply too complex to simulate in a home kitchen.

Once you've got the machine and the supplies, though, cotton candy is a cash cow. A serving of cotton candy, which sells for upward of a dollar, costs only 6 cents to produce, including the cardboard cone. Floss machines start at $600 and can produce 120 servings per hour. At that rate, the machine will pay for itself in just over five hours of brisk business, which is one reason you see so much cotton candy being sold at school and church fairs.

# The Great Debate: Elephant Ears vs. Funnel Cake

Anyone who has been to the fair has faced this dilemma: Should I top off my day at the rides with a funnel cake or an elephant ear? The right answer is a matter of personal taste . . . yet, as always, science is involved.

Funnel cakes are made from a batter of eggs, flour, and water. They were originally created by dripping batter into a vat of boiling oil through a funnel—hence the name. Today, most commercial cakes are made by pouring batter into special metal rings that float in the oil and simulate the funnel's stringy effect. The cake's distinctive shape (like a pile of shoelaces) and the very high heat of the cooking oil make it almost entirely crunchy surface area. This creates great flavor and texture.

Elephant ears are dough, which is why they are sometimes creatively called "fried dough." The difference between a dough and a batter is yeast, which causes dough to rise, and lots more flour, which makes it heavy. Basically, elephant ears are deep- fried, sugary bread. They aren't as flavorful as funnel cakes, but you get more gut-busting volume for the buck. And, you can always slather them in chocolate for a delicious Beaver Tail.

## The Verdict:

If you're hungry or gluttonous, go with elephant ears.

If you're full but tempted, funnel cake is your friend.

If you're on a diet, go home. These calorie-crammed delicacies aren't for you.

# Make it at home:
# Funnel Cakes

Funnel cakes are not only delicious, they're easy to make. The only catch is the oil: ideal cakes are fried at a temperature of about 375 degrees, and hot oil is very dangerous. Be careful. Don't cover the oil with a tight lid. Don't leave the oil unattended. Always experiment before bringing in the children to help.

1 1/3 cup flour

1 1/2 tsp. salt

1/2 tsp. baking soda

2 tbsp. sugar

1/2 tbsp. baking powder

1 tsp. vanilla

1 egg

2/3 cup milk

1. Preheat vegetable oil to 375 degrees.

2. Beat all ingredients together, adding milk until the mixture forms a thick batter that sticks to the beater.

3. The cake can be formed in two ways: funnel cake rings retail for about $30, and come with simple instructions, but it's more fun to use the old-fashioned method of dripping the batter through a funnel in a tight circular twirl. If

you don't have a kitchen funnel, you can cut a hole in the bottom of a Ziploc bag and squeeze the batter through the opening.

4. A great cake is about the size of a pancake. Fry it on one side until the edges are golden and the middle slightly brown. Flip once and fry for another minute. Drain on a paper towel, sprinkle with powdered sugar, and eat while warm.

Yield: 6 servings

# Sno-Cones

Everyone loves a sno-cone (a.k.a. sno-kone) at the amusement park. Crushed ice topped with sickly sweet, neon-colored syrup is the perfect treat on a hot summer day. They're so easy to make, it's almost a crime if you don't try them at home.

Grape juice concentrate and strawberry daiquiri mix make a classic purple and red cone. Blue curacao liquor can be added to lemonade or orange juice concentrate for adults-only green and blue sno-cones. If you want to go authentic, you can purchase carny-cone syrup from the Gold Medal Fun Products Company in handy quart containers.

The key to a perfect sno-cone, though, is the ice. Old-timey sno-cone machines used to grind the ice into pellets the size of rock salt, which caused most of the flavor syrup to drip to the bottom. That was okay for the Dark Ages, but customers are more demanding now. Today's "sno" must be light, fluffy, and capable of holding the syrup. You achieve this consistency not by grinding the ice, but by skimming the "sno" off the surface of a large piece of ice with a sharp blade.

You can make sno-cone ice in a food processor, or you can use one of the dozens of home sno-cone makers on the market. Which one is best? An intrepid reporter from the *Wall Street Journal* asked that very question, and here are his results:

**Most Disappointing**: Hasbro's *Classic Snoopy Snow Cone Machine* is more design than practicality. It features Snoopy napping on his doghouse, out of which flows the crushed ice. Just scoop up the ice shavings with the plastic shovel provided and—wait a second, the crank is difficult to turn, the darn thing falls over constantly, and the chunky ice isn't even tasty.

A misbehaving but lovable childhood friend

**Most Likely To Succeed**: The *Hawaiice Sno Maker* is hand-cranking fun. Even kids can turn the handle with ease, unlike that cranky Snoopy, and the coarse "sno" holds the syrup like a kid clutching a teddy bear. For $23 (and the cost of a little syrup), it will keep you in sugar-highs and brain-freezes until the cold weather hits home.

**Best Overall**: The *Hawaiian Shaved Ice Starter Kit* not only makes a perfectly fluffy "sno," it runs on electricity (no turning that crank!) and comes with brightly colored spoon straws, old-fashioned cups, and some serious sno-cone syrup. But at $54, it will put a pinch on your penny.

# Corn Dogs

A Canadian walks into an American bar. His friend orders him a corn dog. The Canadian is horrified. After much protesting, he agrees to try a bite. He loves it. Turns out, he thought a corn dog was a hot dog with corn inside it.

That's a true story, so in case you're Canadian: A corn dog is a hot dog, on a stick, dipped in a cornbreadlike batter, and fried golden brown.

Corn dogs are a United States original (unlike popcorn, which was eaten by the ancient Incas long before the white man set foot in the New World), and for most of the twentieth century Americans were the only people on earth to eat them. But times they are a'changing, and the rest of the world is catching up. For instance, according to some expertly translated corn dog propaganda from a German website: "The corn dog has it origin already in 1938 in south states of USA and today Americans consume approximately two billion per year . . . Corn dog could be the newest most popular fast food in [German] country!"

As any good German or person from south states of USA knows, the most important element of the corn dog is the batter. Some carnies create their own batter from scratch, but most use one of two commercial mixes: Dipsy Dog or Pronto Pup, both manufactured by the Gold Medal Fun Products Company. Pronto Pup is less sweet than Dipsy Dog, and yes, you can tell the difference.

Beware: Some booths buy frozen corn dogs and just heat them up in an oven or microwave. This simply will not do for the corn dog connoisseur. If you want a lukewarm, spongy dog, you can eat those at home. Good carny dogs are FFB: Fried Fresh

Batter. If you don't see dogs being dipped in thick runny batter and plunged into oil, move on.

Recently, thanks to the uniquely American fat-hating hysteria, baked corn dogs have hit the Midway. Instead of being fried, these dogs are heated in special ovens (like pizza ovens) until golden brown. While these dogs are tastier than their store-bought cousins, they are not to be confused with classic corn dogs. Baked dogs should be avoided unless you are under strict doctor's orders regarding your diet (in which case you should probably avoid carny food altogether).

Even worse than the baked dog is the fate that has befallen the classic wooden corn dog stick. In our overly safety-conscious and litigious society, some moral guardians perceived splinter-or-stabbing danger in the classic wooden rod. The new breed of corn dog sticks are made of tightly rolled paper, putting even the most uptight at ease, but leaving carny food fans with a bit of a bad taste in their mouths.

# Make it at home:
## Corn Dogs

Even if you can't get Dipsy Dog corn dog mix, you can still simulate a carny corn dog at home. The most difficult part is finding a fryer deep enough to hold the dogs straight up and down. Vertical is your only option for great results.

1 cup biscuit mix

1/2 tsp. salt

2 tbsp. yellow cornmeal

1 egg

1/2 cup milk

1. Heat the oil in a fryer to 350 degrees.

2. Mix all the ingredients in a bowl. Blend until smooth, adding water until you get a pancake batter consistency.

3. Stick a skewer in a room temperature hot dog, dip the dog in the batter, let the excess batter drip off for about 5 seconds, then submerge the hot dog (but not the stick) in the oil.

4. Fry until golden brown. Don't even bother to let the dog cool for more than a few seconds before biting right in. Repeat until unable to eat another bite.

For a nice kick, add cayenne pepper or chopped jalapenos to the batter. The equation isn't hard to figure—the more you add, the hotter those doggies get.

For toppings, mix ketchup and mustard in a cup for dipping. Use the end of the corn dog for the mixing. No waste. No worry. Just delicious.

Yield: 8 dogs

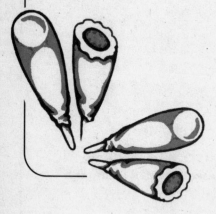

# Food-on-a-Stick

Corn dogs used to be the kings of on-a-stick cuisine, with caramel- and candy-coated apples filling the inferior role of the drunken, half-witted cousin. In the last decade, however, there's been an explosion of the stick-based food group, including:

**Grilled Corn–on–a–Stick**

**Fried Dough–on–a–Stick**

**Cheesecake–on–a–Stick**

**Fried Candy Bars–on–a–Stick**

**Pizza–on–a–Stick**

**Deep-fried Pizza–on–a–Stick**

**Pork Chops–on–a–Stick**

**Deep-fried Twinkies–on–a–Stick**

The secret to turning an ordinary dessert or square of macaroni-and-cheese into a gravity-defying, crowd-pleasing phenomenon is a three-step process (discovered by a clever carny chef, no doubt). First, the on-a-stick object must be frozen. Next, it is coated in flour and rolled in batter to keep the insides from spilling out. Finally, it is flash-fried in very hot oil for about a minute. This technique keeps the center nice and solid, while the edges get runny and delicious beneath their crispy golden shell.

But be warned: Some treats are not what they seem. In many carnivals, the pizza-on-a-stick is simply funnel cake batter sprinkled with cheese flavoring and accompanied by tomato sauce. Deep-fried candy bars sound like heaven, but they're extremely messy and often slide off the stick onto the ground, frustrating many a wide-eyed chocoholic (but pleasing a good many ants).

These disappointments, however, only make the success sweeter. And nothing is sweeter than a fried Twinkie (which is, technically, served on a paper plate instead of a stick, but who's quibbling?). Invented by a Brooklyn restaurateur named Christopher Sell in 2001, the fried Twinkie is sweeping the carnival and fair circuit. One vendor at the 2002 Washington State Fair is rumored to have sold 2,800 fried Twinkies in only three days, about 100 an hour — or 300 pounds a day if calculated in the body fat produced by eating them. With those kinds of numbers you can rest assured that, if they aren't there already, fried Twinkies will soon be making an appearance at your local fair.

Of course, the real thing doesn't come in a box

Admirers describe this new American carnival classic as a kind of soufflé, with the melted white center infusing the fluffy yellow cake with sugary flavor. Skeptics point out the fried variety has three times the calories and six times the fat of an ordinary Twinkie, which isn't exactly a healthy food to begin with. To which Twinkie lovers say: Shut up and live a little! One (or two or three or four) fried Twinkies probably isn't going to kill you!

Like all fried items, fried Twinkies are best eaten warm. Out of the fryer and down the gullet—that's the secret of state fair food.

# Pie in the Sky

One of the great food-related events on the fair circuit is the bake-off. You don't just get to eat it—you get to make it!

But if you think you can just knock off a Betty Crocker special and have a frog hair's chance of winning, you're in for a rude awakening. Most bake-offs are dominated year after year by the same set of women—the kind who enter the cooking contests advertised on the back of cereal boxes and show up all the other mothers at the school bake-off. These eager beavers have not only spent years perfecting their craft, they know exactly what the judges are looking for, which means that if you're going to get your picture in the newspaper with the county's best darn pie, you better know "The Rules."

**Creative Shmee-ative.** Pie-bake contest judges are salt-of-the-earth types, and they prefer simplicity and tradition to groundbreaking works of culinary fancy. An overly creative pie isn't just a waste of time; it's a sure loser.

**The Grandma Plus Factor.** Use a simple recipe, mild spices, and subtle flavoring. Again, the judges aren't looking for a new taste sensation; they're just looking for a pie even better than Grandma used to make.

**Quality Ingredients Matter.** Spend time searching out the very best ingredients in terms of flavor, texture, and color. If they're creating a new apple pie recipe, experts will test at least eight varieties of apples for the best fit. You had better be keeping up.

**Concentrate on the Details.** The winning crust must be light and flaky, but it must also be perfectly fluted (if you choose to flute) and utterly without blemish. Appearance counts!

**Butter, Butter, Butter.** Contest judges love butter.

**The Special Touch.** In a close competition, the little things can make all the difference. Don't go too crazy, but remember that spending ten minutes carving the outline of your home state very carefully into the top of your pie could be the difference between bringing home a ribbon and spending another year listening to Erma brag.

# *Superior Munching Technique*

It goes without saying (although obviously it will be said) that the best food-related carnival contests aren't about baking, they're about eating. As the saying goes: It's better to cram a pie into your face than to put all that time and sweat into baking one.

But, you may ask, why should fat guys get the glory? In a competition full of enormous, swaying bellies, is there any chance for the normal-sized among us? Fret not, Joe Nofatgutson, for your prince has arrived. The best contest eater in the world isn't a rotund bulldozer operator from Dubuque, Iowa, he's a skinny 113-pound Japanese man named Takeru "The Prince" Kobayashi.

Kobayashi, who broke his own world record by eating 50½ hot dogs in 12 minutes at the annual Nathan's hot dog-eating contest on Coney Island, uses a system known as "Superior Munching Technique." Here's the secret:

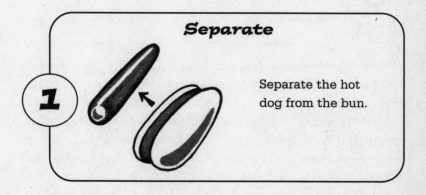

### *Separate*

**1**

Separate the hot dog from the bun.

### Dunk

**2** Tear the bun in half and dunk it in water to compress it. *Do not squeeze it.* Swallow each wet bun half in one bite without chewing. Because of the slipperiness and weight of the water, it should slide right down into your stomach.

### Cram

**3** Break the hot dog in two and line up the halves side by side. Cram both halves into your mouth and power through them in small bites.

**4** Practice, practice, practice! You can't be a world champion overnight, but a few months of practice should make you a local king (or queen).

An alternate method is to skip step 1. Simply tear the dog and bun in half, then dunk them together. Use quick, continuous bites to plow through both halves of the dog and bun at once.

The secret to both methods is the water, which adds weight but decreases volume. This is more than a fair trade-off for a timed event, since stomach area is your biggest concern. Whatever you do, don't drink water during the contest! It's a waste of time and stomach space. Remember: *If it's not dunk, it's not drunk.*

Now that's truly Superior Munching Technique.

# 3

# Milking the Midway: Carnival Games Revealed

Everybody wants to be a hero, and everyone wants to win the prize, but remember one thing— you're on carny turf now, and the carnies are a lot smarter than you are. They know every trick, tactic, and optical illusion.

If it looks easy, it isn't. If it looks impossible, it just might be. If it looks like fun—hey, that's what the carnival is all about.

# The Economics of Play

For vendors, there's only one rule for making money on carny games: *Keep the folks playing.* As long as people are tossing balls or shooting guns, the carnies are winning. It doesn't matter how many giant stuffed dinosaurs it looks like they've given away. In most cases, carnies pocket a profit as soon as you put down your dollar.

The stuffed animals attract the attention, but the most common prizes won at carnival games are combs, rubber ducks, stenciled mirrors, and cheap sunglasses. These low-level prizes cost the carny less than 25 cents to purchase, and often as little as a few pennies apiece. At a buck a game, the carny has locked in a profit of at least 75 cents, even if you win. If they do that several hundred times, they've made their nut, which as you'll recall is the carny technical term for covering expenses.

Sure, combs are for suckers, but what about those stuffed animals? Surely the carny loses money on these prizes, since a medium-sized stuffed animal can retail for as much as $20.

A thousand carnies were asked this question, and ultimately one of them answered it. This carny (who shall remain nameless since he refused to give his name) was running a balloon-pop booth that cost $2 per play. The largest prize that could be won on the first play was a nice-looking, medium-sized stuffed Dalmatian wearing sunglasses and a faux leather coat that would retail for about $15.

A loss for the carny? Of course not. The carny bought his Dalmatians from a warehouse in Brooklyn called Soft Things, Inc., one of about twenty similar operations in the New York City area. Each Dalmatian cost him $1.25. The larger stuffed animals—very impressive-looking prizes that could only be won by winning two games in a row (at a minimum cost of $4)—cost the carny $3.50 each.

In other words, even if a player wins twice in a row, which is highly unlikely, the carny still makes a profit!

The stuffed toys are, of course, knockoffs. That doesn't mean they're not high quality; it just means you're not getting an officially licensed product from a name brand company. Don't believe it? Take a good look at that Sponge Bob Square Pants you just won. He probably doesn't have eyebrows, and his nose isn't quite the same shape as the real Bob's nose. That's why carnies call him "Sponge Bill."

Before you get discouraged or angry or even litigious, keep in mind that your child or love interest will never know you've given them a knockoff (unless they read this book). And besides, you never could have bought that plush "Scooby . . . Doh!" for the carny price. The carny got his knockoffs cheap by placing a bulk order worth several thousand dollars, then splitting the toys with his fellow travelers.

You got the thrill of the victory and a nice souvenir. Isn't that a fair swap?

# The Gaff

Modern carnival games were first developed in the early twentieth century, in the heyday of snake oil salesmen and rain doctors. Most were cheats, designed to take the money off dull-witted rubes and thick-necked farmboys. This worked great on the first few generations of suckers, but by the 1970s a reputation for swindling was killing the business. So carnival booking agents cracked the whip and drove out unscrupulous games. These days, carny games are rarely rigged—or "gaffed," as they say in the carnival—at least not in a way that makes them impossible to win.

If you lose, don't blame the game: 99 percent of the time the loss is your fault. Besides, it's your job to check out the game before you play it. With this book and a careful eye, there's no reason to get suckered by a rigged game, so don't come crying if you get swindled. There may be a sucker born every minute, but it doesn't have to be you.

There are, however, several popular carnival games that are almost always gaffed. Most have been eliminated from the reputable carnival circuit, but you'll still spot an occasional Three Cats or Swinger booth, so listen up.

**Three Cats** (also called Punk Rack) is a simple game involving a ball and three giant stuffed cats. To win, the player has to knock all three cats not just over but *off a table* with three consecutive ball tosses. What the player doesn't realize is that the cats look the same from the front and the back, but because of the distribution of weight they can only be knocked off the table if the front side is facing the player.

To gaff the game, the carny turns one cat around backwards: This makes it impossible to win. The player knocks over the first two cats, but inevitably fails on the third. If the loser questions the game, the carny turns the suspected cat around and shows that it can, in fact, be knocked off the table.

Three Cats can be a fair game, but be smart. If you get two out of three on several consecutive tries, and the carny is egging you on for another round, don't try again! Take your loss like a man, and move on.

In **Swinger,** another classic gaff, a ball is attached to a horizontal pole by a chain or string. The player must swing the ball and knock over a target. The difficulty is that the target must be knocked over not with a direct hit, but by swinging the ball behind the object and knocking it over as the ball swings back toward you.

The gaff is to set the target directly underneath the point where the chain attaches to the pole. Sounds harmless, right? Not when you've got physics to deal with. Here's a lesson:

1. If the object is one inch to the right of the point where the ball is attached, you must arc the ball one inch to

Off-Center: Possible

Centered: Impossible

the left of the point where the ball is attached to knock it over on the return swing. Why? Because the ball will always return the same distance from center that it goes out, but on the opposite side.

2. If the object is directly below the point where the ball is attached, you must throw the ball exactly straight to knock it over on the return swing. But this is impossible, because the object is blocking your path. In order to get the ball behind the object, your initial swing will have to be an arc. The result? Your ball will return in an arc and miss the object completely every time.

Swinger is a classic gaff because, like Three Cats, it is easy to "ungaff" if the carny is questioned. By moving the object an inch to the side, the carny "proves" the game isn't rigged—and the difference in setup isn't obvious to the naked eye. In fact, unscrupulous Swinger carnies will let the sucker win a few practice swings, then gaff the official swing without the player ever suspecting the truth.

A good gaff isn't in the equipment; it's all in the setup.

# The Keys to Winning

The key to winning at carny games is this: Play the right game. Some games are easier to win than others, so know your odds. If two booths have the same game, one is always easier to win. If there's one important thing to learn, it's to watch the game before you put your money down.

**Be the Turtle.** The second key to winning is this: Don't be a hero. The victory goes not to he who throws the hardest, fires the fastest, or looks best in action. Slow, steady, and thoughtful takes home the big prize.

**Keep It Simple.** Never play a game with more than six rules or three ways of winning. For instance, in some games (usually darts) you receive points for doing certain tasks. Each time you pay to play, your points are added to your running total and ultimately redeemed for prizes. The action in these games is rapid-fire, and the scoring intentionally complex. Once you're confused, either by the means of scoring or about your running-point total, you are at the mercy of the carny.

**Play Smart by Playing Dumb.** Never assume you know the rules. Always ask the carny before you start what you have to do to win, how many chances you get, and what prize you will be awarded. The only thing more annoying than spending $20 and losing is finding out you were playing for some crappy frog puppet all along.

**Assume the Worst.** Never forget for a second that the "jointie" (a carny that runs a game booth, which is called a joint) is using every trick in the book to make you fail. Take those basketball-shooting games. Carnies use rims that are smaller than regulation, which are then pounded into ovals to make them appear larger from the front. These days, most rims have a plainly visible sign that says "Not Regulation Diameter." Forewarned is forearmed, right? Not necessarily. There are a thousand other tricks a carny can use to make the game more difficult. They can tilt the backboard or rim. They can attach the rim loosely to the backboard so shots roll off. They can overinflate the basketballs so shots bounce away. They can raise the basket to twelve feet or move the line back farther than a free-throw line.

Even in the fairest basketball games, you can be sure you're using a substandard ball, shooting at a substandard rim, and tossing from a longer distance than it appears. Which means the game is winnable, but difficult. The secret: Shoot "granny style" (underhand). It may not look cool, but it's the best way to counter the carny effect.

Now, here are the secrets to winning a few of the other most popular carnival games.

# The Guessing Game

**RATING: EASY**
**CHANCE OF WINNING: 1 IN 5**

Many people suspect that guessing games, where an expert guesses a fact about you, are rigged. Believe it or not, they aren't. These guys don't cheat; they've just had a lot of practice.

Unless you're unusually built, guessing your weight within five pounds isn't that hard, especially when you've made thousands of guesses in your career. The guesser may feel your muscles or check your height, but he always bases his guess on looking at you. The grabbing is just part of the show, which is why a woman should never let a male weight guesser touch her body.

The age-guessing game uses the same principle: It's all experience. If, for some reason, the guesser is stumped, he just checks out your companions. You may not look twenty-six (your actual age), but if all three of your friends do, you're probably going to lose.

The birth month–guessing game works on a slightly different principle, since (contrary to rumor) birth month doesn't affect your appearance. If the "correct" range is within two months of your actual birth month, the guesser has a 5 in 12 chance of getting the answer right. That's almost 50 percent! The percentage of right guesses is even higher because some nimrods have their birthstones clearly visible on a ring or necklace. These yahoos are always unduly impressed when the pro guesses right.

There is one scam associated with the birth month–guessing game. If the expert writes down a month beforehand to show you after you've told him your birth date, always say your birth month is October. Why? Because the carny always writes down the same thing—a handwritten squiggle that can pass for Jan (for January), June, or July. With those three months to choose from, and a two-month window on each side of the right month, the carny has all the months of the year covered—except October!

This scam is extremely rare, however. In most cases, about 20 percent of people win the guessing game, and the carny goes away happy because the prize awarded to winners costs less than the price of playing. That's why this game isn't about right and wrong answers, as anyone who's seen *The Jerk* knows, it's about putting on a show and having some good clean fun.

# *Darts*

It doesn't matter how many bull's-eyes you hit down at the local bar, or how much you practice in your basement rec room—it's not going to help you once you hit the carnival.  Why? Because dart games rely heavily on the quality of the darts, and carny darts are mangled, sawed-off monstrosities. In fact, the better your technique the worse they fly, so leave your stylish wrist flick in the beer hall.

Wooden carny darts always have a few feathers that have been whittled down, making them curve during flight. Plastic carny darts are either too light to fly accurately, or so front-heavy they dive down and away from the target. Even worse, carny darts are notoriously dull, and many have such weak points that they won't penetrate the target, no matter how accurately you throw them.

The most popular dart game, **Hit the Star**, also relies on a visual illusion. The stars look large and easy to hit because they have long thin arms. In reality, the winning areas (the arms) are so slim, and the blank spaces between them so wide, that even when you get within the star's diameter your chance of winning is only about 5 percent (1 in 20). You're better off playing at a booth with small, compact stars, but even these games are built to fool you because the winning area is smaller than a regulation bull's-eye.

64

Don't be fooled: All stars are not the same

If you must play darts, play **Balloon Pop**. If you pop a balloon, you win the prize written on the tab behind it. What could be simpler? The game looks easy because the board is covered with balloons, but remember that the darts are dull so you have to hit the balloons right in the center to pop them. The secret is always to aim for a shiny, translucent balloon. These balloons are fully inflated; the dull, underinflated balloons will cause the dart, and your chance of winning, to bounce harmlessly away.

The reason people win at Balloon Pop is because most of the prizes are of the plastic comb variety. Insider wisdom says the big prizes are hidden along the edge of the board, but carnies aren't stupid. They know you think you have it all figured out. Your best bet is to aim for the top of the board, near the corners. Most people naturally err on the low side, so the high side "dead zones" are your best chance to get lucky and win that Harley-Davidson vanity mirror.

# Pyramid

RATING: VERY DIFFICULT
CHANCE OF WINNING: 1 IN 200

Almost every carnival has Pyramid (also known as Spill the Milk), in which three stacked metal bottles must be knocked off a table with one throw. If ever a game was known for the gaff, it's Pyramid. Jokes abound about hurricanes not being able to knock the bottles over. And yet, the masochists continue to play.

The truth is, in the old days Pyramid was a rigged game. The classic gaff is to fill one or more of the bottles with so much lead that it can't be knocked over with the ultra-light softball the contestant throws. Simple, yes, but too easily detectable by the local vice officer.

A more sophisticated gaff involves pouring molten lead into one side of a bottle. A lopsided bottle won't roll, so it can be knocked over, but not off the table. This gaff is especially effective because many contestants don't understand that they must knock the bottle off the table to win. Again, the vice squad can easily detect this fraud.

The most efficient trick, and the one that's given this game a bad name, is a basically unprovable gaff. It involves having one bottle that is heavier than the others, but light enough to be knocked off the table by a direct hit.

The carny, who knows his bottles like his pack of cigarettes, can make the game impossible to win by setting the heavy bottle on the bottom row, *slightly behind* a lighter bottle. In this setup, a perfect throw will hit the lighter bottle first; when the ball reaches the heavy bottle, it won't have enough momentum to knock it off the table.

66

The winning spot ... in an honest game

Like all great gaffs, the trick is all in the setup. If the carny wants to prove the game is winnable, he puts the heavy bottle on the top of the pyramid, which makes the game easy to win.

In other words, with Pyramid you can easily find yourself at the mercy of the carny, and that's clearly not the best place to be. You're much better off playing a throwing game where you have to knock over a series of objects, like Coke bottles, pegs, or records. These games are difficult because they require several good throws, but they're very straightforward and almost never rigged.

Still willing to take a chance on Pyramid? Then the advice is pretty simple: Cross your fingers and hope for an honest setup, then throw a ball that hits all three bottles at the same time. To do this, aim for the triangular zone where the three bottles meet. A winning throw will just clip the bottom of the top bottle, with most of the force hitting the bottom two legs of the pyramid.

A common Pyramid scheme is to bounce the throw in the hopes of getting a better angle. A carny must have started this myth, because the bounced throw is a loser every time.

# Shoot Out the Star

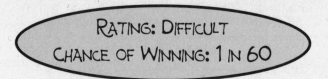

RATING: DIFFICULT
CHANCE OF WINNING: 1 IN 60

Shooting games are a classic of the Midway, and are about as much fun as you can have without putting your eye out. But they are not easy to win.

Most customers worry about the bend in the gun barrels. It's true: The guns are old, cheap, and crooked as elbows. However, in a multiple-shot game this defect can be overcome once you take your first shot, because the bend is the same every time and you can compensate for it.

The biggest problems in the shooting games are the BBs, which have usually been shot so many times they've practically been hammered into squares. Dents cause the BBs to fire in unpredictable directions. C'est la vie. This is the carnival, not the country club's skeet-shooting range.

In Shoot Out the Star, one of the most popular carnival games of all time, the object is to shoot out every piece of a red star on a target with 100 BBs. It's a difficult task, but not impossible—if you've got the right target.

Always check the target before shooting. If the star is bigger than 1½ inches in diameter, your chance of winning is less than 1 in 1000. Always look for the game with the smallest star, and remember to check the paper quality. If it's linen or perforated, your job just got much tougher.

Once you've found the best shooting booth, the strategy is this: Shoot a circle around the star and knock it out in one big piece. To win, you have to create a complete circle with no gaps.

Even if you know the strategy, you'll need at least a 90 percent shooting accuracy to accomplish this task.

Don't ever try to hit the star itself. Any shot that hits the star is a wasted shot, because you don't have enough BBs to shoot away the entire star piece by piece. It may look like a winner, but you'll always end up having a little piece of red hanging on at the end.

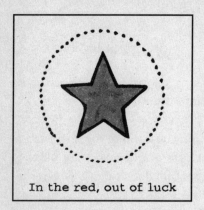

In the red, out of luck

The secret within the secret is to go slow. Do not fire off all your shots at once. Fire 3 to 5 BBs at a burst, then check where they've hit *without moving the gun or your arms.* Keep firing in short bursts, checking your results, and realigning your shot. Slow and steady definitely wins this race.

Don't assume you've won until it's verified by the carny. Many an unhappy customer has wasted their last twenty "victory" shots only to discover that a little bit of red stood between them and that big plush bear.

# Shoot the Freak

A new development on the Midway are games in which the contestant doesn't win a prize, no matter how well he performs. These games are played for the thrill of the moment, not the lure of possessions.

Of the new breed of games—let's call them Sure Losers—the most popular are speed pitch and paintball. Most setups are harmless, but like anything else they can easily spiral out of control, as one did recently on the Coney Island boardwalk.

It was the middle of July when some clever but cruel entrepreneur converted a vacant, garbage-strewn lot into a money machine with a simple concept: A person on the boardwalk got three paintball shots at a "freak" taunting them from the lot below. The game was called Shoot the Freak.

Paintballs hurt, and the distance was only about twenty feet, so the person in the lot wore bulky, space suit-like, full-body protection. Unfortunately, it was 100 degrees that July. The suit must have been stifling, because within an hour the poor guy was slumped in a metal folding chair in the middle of the lot, barely able to weave from side to side. That didn't keep a continuous line of young men from pumping paintballs into the almost comatose target.

Shoot the Freak: A new low in American entertainment.

# Milk Can Toss

**RATING: EASY**
**CHANCE OF WINNING: 1 IN 5**

No, this isn't a game where you actually get to toss milk cans, as cool as that sounds. In the Milk Can Toss, the tossing is done with a softball, which you have to throw into an old-fashioned 10-gallon metal milk can. The catch: The hole is only one-sixteenth of an inch larger than the softball.

Sound difficult? The answer is both yes and no. The Milk Can Toss is one of the easier games to win, *if* you practice, and *if* you know what you're doing. It also yields some of the biggest prizes on the Midway, so here's your chance to make a good impression on that cute girl you met in the line for the Ferris wheel.

Conventional wisdom tells you to lob the ball as high as you can, since this gives you a better angle for landing the ball directly in the hole. Carnies know this is the most common strategy, so they usually hang the big prizes right over the cans to prevent you from throwing the skyball.

That's fine, because a high toss is not the secret to this game. The skyball helps only if you hit directly in the hole. This is possible, but improbable. Remember: The hole is only one-sixteenth of an inch wider than the ball.

The best way to win this game is toss the ball so that it goes in either when it hits the hole *or* when it hits the edge of the hole. Stop now and take note: For this strategy to work, you must make sure the milk can you're aiming for has a top that slopes into the hole.

Even with these sloped cans, a normal throw will bounce right off the rim. The key is to cut the momentum of the toss with backspin. Here's the secret: Use an underhand tossing motion, but grip the ball on top instead of underneath. As you release the ball, flick your wrist upward—this creates the proper spin.

The second key is to throw the ball softly, but without much arc. Because of the angle of trajectory, a low-arc shot will never go directly into the hole. However, a soft low toss combined with backspin will usually bounce back into the hole if you hit either the front lip of the can or the sloped edge behind the hole.

Nothing will help if your ball hits to the side of the hole. Those shots are losers, so always make sure you've got the correct line.

Even with these tips, your margin of error is small, so start practicing. All you need is a regulation softball and a hole 4 inches in diameter, preferably cut into something hard, like a

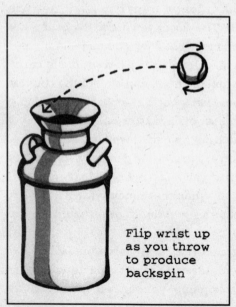

Flip wrist up as you throw to produce backspin

piece of plywood. Make sure to set the target at the height of your shoulder, since this is how the milk cans will be set up at the carnival. Once you're able to throw the ball consistently either in the hole or off the front or back edge of the hole, you're only a few tosses (and a few bucks) away from being a big winner.

# Whiffle Ball Toss

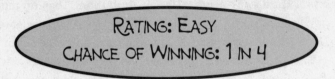

RATING: EASY
CHANCE OF WINNING: 1 IN 4

In Whiffle Ball Toss (sometimes called Flukey), you must bank a whiffle ball off a slanted board and into a basket. The size of the board, size of the basket, angle of the board, and distance to the target will vary from game to game. Some carnies allow leaning, while others make a player stand straight behind a line. The difficulty depends on all these factors in combination, so there's only one way to make sure the game is fair—ask the carny to play it.

When asked, most carnies will quickly toss in a winner from their side of the counter. Nice try, carny guy, but there's one truth common to all setups: The closer you are to the board, the better your chance of winning. That's why you should always lean over as far as possible, if leaning is allowed. If the carny can't prove the game is winnable from your side of the counter with a legal throw, the game isn't worth the price of his whiffle balls (which cost about 5 cents each wholesale).

You also have to watch out for gaffed whiffles. The heavier the ball, the more likely you are to win the game. Unscrupulous carnies use a taped or stuffed ball when giving a demonstration or letting you practice. Then, when the money's down, it's back to the lightweight, undoctored whiffle. In other words, keep your eye on the ball!

But if you just watched the carny prove his skills, and you're sure the balls are regulation weight, you've learned a valuable lesson: To win this game, you must toss the ball as lightly as possible and barely graze the board.

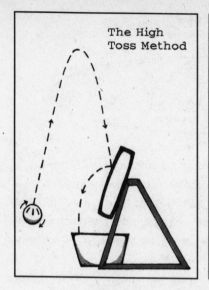

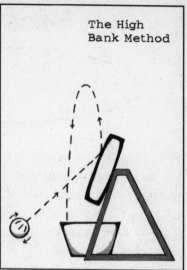

This can be done in two ways. The first is to hit near the top of the board as the ball is *on the way up*. This is the best method when you are within 3 feet of the board, either because the throwing line is close or you are allowed to lean. The second option is to toss the ball high and short, causing it to hit near the middle of the board *on the way down*.

In both methods, the key is to start the throw as low as you can. This allows the ball to get more vertical (up and down) flight than horizontal (front to back) flight. Get as close to the board as possible, bend over as far toward the ground as allowed, and always use an underhand toss.

The last element of a successful toss is front-spin. This is the opposite of the spin employed in the Milk Can Toss and is created by holding your hand under the ball. As you release, flick your wrist backwards (toward your body), brushing your fingertips along the bottom and back edge of the ball. Be gentle. A winning throw will feel like it slipped off your fingertips, but it will end with the sweet "thwonk" of success.

# Ring Toss

Ring Toss is one of the oldest games on the Midway. It's also one of the most difficult. It looks easy when you see those hundreds of Coke bottles stacked together in a square, but it's not. In fact, the odds of winning this game have been calculated to be as high as 600 to 1. No wonder they give you so many rings for two dollars!

Aiming for one bottle and trying to loft a ring around it will never work. That's why this game is primarily a game of chance. At these odds, you're better off with the lottery than using the "precise toss" method.

The problem is that the rings aren't much bigger than the bottles. Even worse, the rings are so light that when you do ring a bottle with a direct hit, they always bounce off. The heavier the rings, the better your chance of success—this is the

Ricochet for a ringer... or forget this game

most important calculation when considering where to spend your dollar.

Of course, as you know by now, there's always a way to increase your odds—in this case, all the way down to 1 in 200! The secret is to throw a ricochet.

The best way to throw a ricochet is to toss the ring sidearm, like a Frisbee. When you release it, get as close to the level of the tops of the bottles as possible. Most bottles are set well below the level of the counter to thwart this strategy, but bend over as far as you can. The more parallel you are to your target, the more action your ring will get.

The concept is similar to skipping a rock on a lake. Your goal is to skip the ring off the bottles as many times as you can. Hopefully, the ring will slow down enough by the last ricochet to simply fall over a bottle without enough momentum to bounce off it.

# Ping-Pong Goldfish

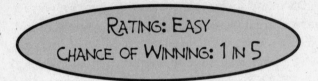

RATING: EASY
CHANCE OF WINNING: 1 IN 5

When many humans think of childhood, they inevitably remember standing in a room at their church or elementary school trying to throw a Ping-Pong ball into a jar to win a goldfish. And what parent hasn't agonized over having to flush the dear departed pet down the toilet two days later? It's as close to a universal experience as carnival games get.

The reason for the immense popularity of this game is, of course, the goldfish. Baby goldfish cost about 10 cents apiece, and they're convenient for small carnivals because they can be bought at any pet store. Even better, kids go absolutely crazy for them.

The other secret to its popularity is that the game is winnable, even for small children. Why? Because it's mostly luck—but with fairly high odds of success.

Ping-Pong Goldfish is a cross between a skill game like Milk Can Toss and a game of chance like Ring Toss. As in Ring Toss, the Ping-Pong balls are so light that they tend to bounce off the edges of the containers and out of the playing area, leading to many an unhappy first-grader.

But unlike Ring Toss, where even accurate throws bounce off and become losers, if the Ping-Pong ball hits directly in the jar it will stay. The reason: Water. A Ping-Pong ball will not bounce out of water; therefore, if your ball touches water, it's a winner.

The proper technique for Ping-Pong Goldfish is to choose a specific jar and shoot for the center of it. Always shoot for a jar in the middle of the playing area, because if your shot bounces off the intended target it has a better chance to land in a nearby jar.

And that's where the good luck kicks in. Or, for the parent who must now make a home for Goldie the Death-Prone Goldfish, the bad luck.

# The Test of Strength

RATING: VARIES
CHANCE OF WINNING: GUARANTEED
(IN THE RIGHT CONDITIONS) ✱

The Test of Strength, referred to in the carnival as High Striker, is one of the carny's great inventions. It's the he-man game, the game of show-offs, the ultimate competition between friends. In other words, it punches all the right buttons and keeps the money flowing. Even better for the carny, pride is usually the only prize.

It's also a game that can easily be won, even by the weakest member of your posse, as long as the conditions are right. After all, you're not actually lifting weights; you're just hitting a pad with a mallet.

The secret of this game is not strength; it's swing accuracy. The mallet must hit the pad directly for you to have a snowball's chance in summer of ringing that gong. The best stroke is the overhand swing, where you put your whole body into it. This is exactly the stroke you use when you chop wood. As anyone who's ever chopped wood knows, perfecting this motion, and achieving accuracy, is much harder than it seems. If you know how to chop wood and your friends don't, you have a very good chance of wiping the floor with their sorry butts.

The second sure way to win, even if you're a weakling, is to know the gaff. All High Striker games manufactured in the last twenty years are extremely fair. However, there are many older

✱ Unless you're a total wimp.

versions floating around that put you entirely at the mercy of the carny.

In the old version of High Striker, the weight runs up a wire when the pallet is struck. Unknown to most players, this

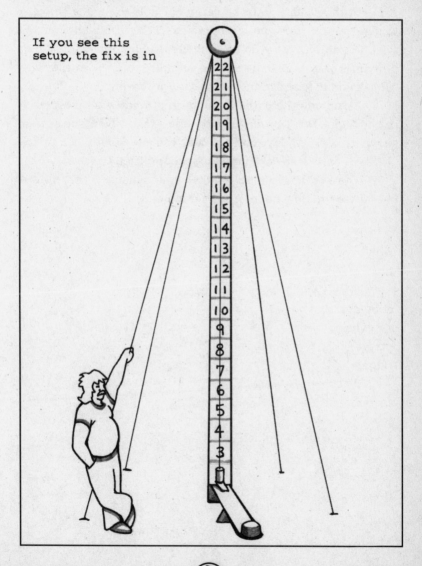

If you see this
setup, the fix is in

wire doesn't just run to the top—it then loops behind the bell and down to the ground to help hold the structure in place. From there it's simple physics: The bell cannot be rung if this wire is loose. When the wire is tight, the game is easy to win.

In the classic gaff, the carny controls the game through this seemingly innocent support wire. When he wants you to win, he tightens the wire by casually leaning against it. When he wants you to lose, he stands up and the slack in the wire causes you to look like the world's biggest wimp.

If you see the carny leaning on a guide wire, suspect a rigged game. Don't turn him in, though—take advantage of your knowledge. A simple payoff can keep the wire tight when you're playing—and loose for your unsuspecting friends.

The result: No matter what your muscle mass, you're guaranteed to be a he-man among mortals.

# The Rope Ladder

RATING: EASY

CHANCE OF WINNING: 1 IN 3
(IF YOU PRACTICE AT HOME)

In this game, formerly known as Indian Rope Trick, the player must climb a nine-rung rope ladder and ring a bell at the top. The difficulty lies in the ladder, which is suspended on both ends by pivoting pulleys, so that as soon as you misstep you get spun over and thrown to the mat.

Rope Ladder is a game of pure skill, as any rope carny will be happy to demonstrate by scampering up the ladder and ringing the bell with ease. Don't get discouraged: It took the carny hundreds of hours of practice to learn to climb that ladder. You can learn it in a mere fifty or so.

The secret is balance. You must be perfectly balanced at all times, or you're going to get dumped. The first key is to get your center of gravity as wide as possible. Place your feet on the corner where the rung meets the ladder. Place your hands on the *outside* rope, between the rungs. Your weight will press down on these ropes, stabilizing them as you wait.

Now comes the hard part: Moving. You must counterbalance every movement on the left side of your body with a movement on the right. When you lift your left foot and move it to the next rung, you must *simultaneously* lift and move your right (opposite) arm the same distance. Humans do not move this way naturally—our instinct is to reach with the hand then move the foot—so the "two-sided stretch" is awkward and difficult to perform without practice (see how in the following sidebar, "Make it at home: The Rope Ladder").

If you learn the technique correctly, you'll be able to move quickly, with your weight forward at all times. If you lean back or make a sudden motion on the ladder, you're screwed. The same is true if you catch a foot or knee on the rope while moving, so always keep your toes pointed out (not down) and point your knees to the outside.

If you can do these things, and do them well, you'll be a man, my son (or my daughter).

# Make it at home:
## The Rope Ladder

Being able to climb the rope ladder is the coolest skill at the amusement park. It will amaze your friends, embarrass your enemies (when they fall off), and impress your secret love. The key is to perfect the "two-sided stretch" walking technique. And the best part is, once you've mastered the motion, you can climb the ladder every time. That's why most carnies limit you to one win per day.

You don't need a rope ladder suspended over a mat to practice the Rope Ladder at home. You simply need two bricks and a standard, one-piece wood ladder: The kind made to lean against the wall, not a fold-out ladder that will stand up on its own. If you're practicing over a hard floor, like a concrete garage, some padding under the ladder is also recommended.

1. Begin by getting down on all fours on the floor. Move your right hand and left foot simultaneously. Make sure not to cross your legs in front of your feet, and to keep your arms and legs the same distance apart as you walk across the floor. That's not so hard, is it?

2. Now lay the ladder flat on the floor. Stand on it with your feet on the outside corner

of the bottom rung and your hands halfway between the second and third rungs. Got it? Good. Now use the "two-sided stretch" to walk to the other end.

3. When you're able to "walk" the ladder ten times in a row, place a brick under the exact middle of the last rung, with the long side facing you. Climb on (make sure your fingers aren't wrapped underneath the ladder) and try to do the "two-sided stretch" to the top. The ladder will tip from side to side and touch the floor. If you'd been on a rope ladder, you would have just been dumped off.

4. Once you've walked the ladder ten times in a row without an edge touching the ground, place a second brick under the first rung, elevating the whole ladder off the floor. When you've mastered that stage, turn the bricks so that their narrow end faces you. The next and last step is to set the bricks upright on their sides.

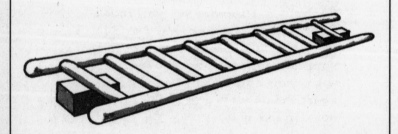

If you can master the bricks on their sides, you stand a reasonable chance of winning at Rope Ladder. But don't expect instant success. The actual game is more difficult than your

practice ladder for three reasons: 1) rope is more difficult to climb than wood; 2) the carny ladder is sloped at an upward angle; and 3) the game's pivot point is smaller than even the narrowest side of your brick.

Don't get discouraged. A few rounds on the carny ladder and you'll get the hang of it. And once you win a few times, you'll be a winner for life.

# The Water Gun Race

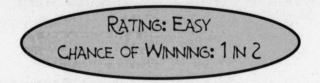

RATING: EASY
CHANCE OF WINNING: 1 IN 2

The Water Gun Race is a test of skill and machinery—but mostly machinery. Since this game doesn't involve strength or balance, and is never gaffed, it's the perfect game for family, friends, or even couples on an old-fashioned first date.

In Water Gun Races, every round produces a winner. Go for a round with only a few players, right? Wrong. In most games, the size of the prize is based on the number of participants in the race. You should therefore always try to play in a full game. Why? Because with this book you have a distinct advantage over the uninformed.

Please don't enter a game against children. Only jerks pick on kids. Besides, they'll probably beat you, and then you'll really look like a horse's rear.

The secret to winning a Water Gun Race, be it clown head, racehorse, or other miscellaneous variety, is choosing the right nozzle. The race is won in the first 3 seconds, so you must grab the early advantage.

Don't go for the nozzle with the hardest spray. The strength with which the water hits the button doesn't matter—the key is consistency. You want the water spray that reaches the button first. Ironically, this will be the nozzle with the least amount of water pressure (unless you find a real dud where the water won't even reach the target). Watch a few rounds before playing, and you'll spot the winning hose.

If you've chosen the right nozzle, you've got the advantage. Now the key is getting to the button first—and staying there. The secret: Start out aiming 2 inches above the button. As the pressure rises, the water stream will rise toward the target. When your button is hit, move your aim slowly downward to counter the rising water pressure.

After 3 seconds, you will be at full strength. At that point, if you're not on the button you're a loser. If you've played the game right, though, you should be in the lead. Just keep her steady now, partner, and you're off to the winner's circle.

# Hanky-Panks

Hanky–panks are games that guarantee the player a win. Of course, most of the prizes are lousy. The carny's goal is to get you to keep playing the game, and plunking down cash, until you get enough credits to trade up to a better prize. For this reason, hanky–panks are commonly referred to as trade–ups.

The classic hanky–pank is **Duck Pond** (sometimes played as Fish Pond). In this game, you pay to pick a rubber duck floating in a plastic kiddie pool. Your prize is determined by the tag on the bottom of your duck. In most games, about 70 percent of the ducks yield the smallest prize, which is . . . a rubber duck!

Dart and ball hanky–panks allow the player to throw until they win. A classic example is the game in which you keep throwing darts until you pop a balloon, then win the prize written on the tag behind it.

Even games like **Skee-Ball** or **Whack-a-Mole** are considered hanky–panks. Yes, the player gets tickets based on their score—in other words, their skill—but you always have to play dozens of games before moving beyond the plastic comb or pencil prize level. That's why games like Skee-Ball should never be played for profit. This hanky–pank is simply good clean fun.

Despite their seemingly harmless nature, there have been several attempts to shut down hanky–panks. In 1973, the Illinois Attorney General tried to close down the Duck Pond at the state fair, claiming that because the game awarded prizes based entirely on luck it was an illegal lottery. After a public outcry, and a few minor changes, the game was reinstated.

The truth is this: Duck Pond is not an illegal lottery; it is a game for children. Adults who try to win big prizes at hanky–panks are desperate, stupid, or both.

# Buildup Games

**RATING: EASY (BUT WITH A PRICE)**
**CHANCE OF WINNING: 1 IN 2**

Buildup games are the evil, cigarette-smoking cousins of the mild-mannered hanky–panks. While hanky–panks are fun to hang around with, you must always, always resist the temptation to go down a dark alley with a buildup game.

In a buildup, the odds of successfully completing the task, often either by throwing a ball through a hoop or hitting a balloon with a dart, are about 1 in 2. But when the player wins, they don't get the nice prize prominently displayed. They get the cheap trinket hidden behind the counter. In carny speak, these prizes are known as "scum."

In order to get the nice prizes, the player is told, he must win a certain number of games. Only now does the player realize that, at 50-50 odds on each play, he's going to have to spend a lot of money to win that wonder toy for his adoring child.

At this point, a sly carny will usually offer the player a break, such as making a shot for him or lowering the threshold to win the nice prize. That, my friend, is the buildup. Don't fall for it—it's a trap! You will soon have spent so much money that you'll feel compelled to push on to the big prizes, even if it means you won't be able to make the next payment on your truck.

The best way to avoid a buildup is to watch the game before playing it. Since every other person who plays wins scum (remember that the odds of success are about 50-50), this rigged game is by far the easiest to spot.

If you get suckered, just take your scum and leave the area. Better to walk away with a plastic comb and some dignity than a plush stuffed bear and a second mortgage on your house.

# 4

# THRILLS, CHILLS, AND KILLS: CARNIVAL RIDES REVEALED

There is no denying it: The rides are the main attraction of the amusement park. No matter how old you are, there is nothing better than seeing the top of a roller coaster come into view across ten lanes of traffic.

Actually, there is one thing better: Climbing on board.

# Amused to Death?

Make no mistake: Amusement parks and carnivals are one of America's safest recreational activities. According to the National Consumer Product Safety Commission, only about 7,000 of the estimated 270 million annual visitors to amusement parks sustain emergency-room level injuries. That's less than 1 in every 38,500 people. Rides cycle at least 100 times per day, so that's about one injury in every 40 million rides. Which means you have less than a one in a million chance of sustaining a life-threatening injury while riding the Vortex.

But what about actual deaths? Between 1972 and 1997, there were 114 deaths from accidents at amusement parks, carnivals, fairs, fun centers, and water parks—just over four a year. Thirty-three of those deaths occurred on roller coasters, and almost half of those killed were employees performing maintenance. The worst disaster in the last fifty years, which killed eight teenagers at Six Flags Great Adventure in the 1980s, didn't have anything to do with falls, thrills, or speed. Instead, the tragedy was the result of a fire caused by a defective lightbulb in a haunted house.

In other words, you are in far more danger of getting injured or killed while driving to the amusement park than you are at the park itself.

The problem, from a public relations standpoint, is that amusement park deaths—usually involving crushing, massive head trauma, severe spinal injury, or other body-mangling disasters—make good media stories. That's why ordinary people not only hear about them, they remember them.

Many of these blood-curdling accidents are the result of customer misconduct. The easiest way to die on a ride is to unbuckle your seat belt or unlock the safety bar. Standing up on a roller coaster, especially at the top of the big hill, is a cheap ticket to the afterlife.

Preexisting medical conditions are also a common killer. Most involve the heart or brain. There's been more than one instance where a person suffered instant death on a roller coaster because of a brain aneurysm, the fancy scientific term for a big sac of blood in your head just waiting to explode under the right conditions—like hurtling down a hill into an upside-down loop at about 80 miles per hour.

In order to keep you alive (and spending money), amusement parks and carnivals have come up with standard rules and requirements for dangerous rides. These rules are printed on signs, then promptly ignored by customers. Yet, there is wisdom to be gained here. And what else do you have to do while waiting in line for more than an hour? So pay attention!

- **Bad brains.** If the sign says don't ride if you have a heart or brain condition, and you have said condition, don't ride!

- Child's play. Parks often won't let kids ride without a parent. That's because unsupervised kids do stupid things, like dare each other to stand up on roller coasters. This has happened at least ten times in recent decades, leading to ten deaths. In other words, this rule is fair. If you're younger than the minimum age, bring a parent—or at least an adult posing as your parent. It's uncool, but it's better than a body cast.

- **No short people.** The problem here is that small people can slip out from under lap bars or not fit correctly into the shoulder restraints. For the most part, though, parks are overly cautious. If you know you're barely shorter than the minimum required for some rides, think ahead and wear shoes that make you taller. Then make every effort to bypass the sign altogether. Walk casually past, as far from the sign as possible, as if height isn't a question.

If the carny insists on a measurement, rock up on your toes as you step up to the sign. Don't go all the way to tiptoes—that's too obvious! If you still miss the mark, the carny may take pity and let you ride. If he doesn't, that's a sure sign the danger is real. Always heed the wisdom of the carny.

- **Crushed by a big man.** If a ride (such as The Scrambler) swings around a central pivot, centrifugal force will push the riders toward the outside of the spin, causing the far rider to absorb the impact of the weight of the inside rider. This is only a problem if *the difference in weight is more than 70 pounds*. If this is the case, always heed the warnings and put the big rider on the outside. A parent seriously injuring his or her small child, as happened when a four-year-old girl was crushed (but not killed) by her mother on the Starfish at Six Flags Marine World, is a sure path to long-term psychological torment.

# Keep Hands and Feet Inside the Vehicle at All Times

Keep hands and feet inside the vehicle at all times: Is there a more well-known safety warning? The phrase, like many in the carnival, has become a cliché, used by everyone from parents disciplining their children to high school students getting ready to take final exams.

But why? Was there a time when hands and feet were routinely sliced off reckless passengers by steel bars, flying metal, or loose boards? Is the story of two nuns being decapitated on that local roller coaster in the 1960s really true?

The answer is no. While it is easy to uncover documentation on deaths and maimings at American amusement parks and carnivals, none involve the loss of protruding body parts (including heads). Ride designers are smart people, and they wouldn't design a ride in which limb loss is even a remote possibility. These designers understand a fundamental truth: If you give people a chance to do something stupid, even the tiniest chance, someone will do it.

Many rides play into this fear. Roller coasters, for instance, will swing close to an overhanging part or dip down just before entering a tunnel, making you think you're about to lose an arm. No one ever does.

That doesn't mean the warning should be ignored. It's there for an important reason: If you have your hands and feet inside the car at all times, you won't be able to do something truly dangerous like lean out of the car, stand up, or commit any other act to cause your own bloody demise.

And remember: Although headless nuns are common in carnival-related urban legends, no nun has ever been killed in an American amusement park accident. If nuns were decapitated while riding a roller coaster (God forbid!), you can rest assured no one would ever ride that coaster again.

# How to Spot a Spine-Cracker

Most rides are safe. If that statement is true, which it is, then by definition some rides are not safe. The last thing even the cheapest amusement park or carnival wants is to hurt someone, so their inspectors can generally be trusted to check the construction, electrical systems, engineering, and operation of the rides. Still, even the carnival isn't immune to laziness, corruption, and greed, and as you know some states never bother to inspect amusement park rides at all.

So how can you tell if that metal monstrosity is a safe ride? Surprisingly, outward appearances aren't necessarily the best gauge. For instance, many people worry about old rides, like The Spider or The Monster, which both feature large, old-fashioned lightbulbs along their wooden arms (you'll know them when you see them). In reality, these rides are often the safest on the lot. Older rides are very well manufactured, and if they've made it this long the operator has put a lot of time and care into them.

The secret to spotting a spine-cracker is to look behind the attraction before riding it. Everybody keeps the front looking nice—it's the back of the ride that tells the true story. With that in mind, here are a few tips from the experts for spotting the turkeys before they rupture your vertebrae:

- **Follow the electrical lines.**
  If you see broken wires, loose connections, or poor groundings (such as wires lying in a puddle of water), that's an unsafe ride.

- **Check the blocking.** The ground beneath portable rides is almost always uneven, so operators use blocks to make the ride level. If the blocking looks flimsy, cheap, or ill-conceived, you can be sure that's not the only problem.

- **Look under the hood.** Unscrupulous ride owners have been known to repair faults they think are hidden from view using aluminum foil, sticks, scrap metal, or even a screwdriver shoved into a crack or between parts.

- **Inspect the paint.** If the paint is old and worn but shows a few nice, fresh spots, it could mean the owner has painted over cracks or other structural problems.

Remember: A dirty ride doesn't mean it's unsafe. A ride jockey who needs a haircut or shower isn't necessarily a poor or inattentive operator. However, these factors are a tip-off. You wouldn't eat at a restaurant with dirty tables, floors, or counter areas: It's just not kosher. The same holds true for a carnival company. Their product is good, clean, safe fun. Make sure the environment they provide is conducive to that goal.

# Operator Error: The B&B Himalaya Tragedy

At the 1998 Austin-Travis County Livestock Show & Rodeo, a fifteen-year-old-girl was killed on the Himalaya, a common ride that involves cars on a loop track spinning over a series of small hills while disco music blasts in the background. As an investigation would prove, the girl's lap bar broke as she neared the top of a hill, causing her to fly from her seat and slam into the back wall of the ride. She died almost instantly from massive chest, neck, and head trauma.

Immediately after the incident, the ride was declared safe by carnival operators. The responsible safety inspector, who had examined the ride ten days earlier, said it was impossible for the bar to have broken off, despite the fact that the girl was still clutching it when she died.

In truth, the ride had been cited eight previous times for safety violations. A month earlier, California safety officials had raided the Del Mar Fair to shut the ride down, but by the time they arrived the Himalaya and its operator had slipped out of town.

In addition to the faulty lap bar, the post-accident investigation found twelve other serious safety hazards on the ride. They also found that the owner was aware of the safety violations and the ride had knowingly been operated at an unsafe speed.

In November 2000, the owner of B&B Amusements pleaded guilty to manslaughter charges on behalf of himself and the company. He was the first ride operator convicted of negligent homicide.

In May 2001, the inspector who had deemed the ride safe, despite the long list of problems and complaints, also pleaded guilty to manslaughter charges. He had been a member of the board of directors of the National Association of Amusement Park Safety Officials, and only months before had been given the organization's "Man of the Century" award for his dedication to ride safety.

# Don't Drink the Water: The Log Ride

The Log Ride (also known as the Flume, a term that originally referred to a narrow shoot used to transport logs down rivers) is an amusement park classic . . . despite the fact that the first one, the Log Flume at Six Flags Over Texas, didn't open until 1963. The Log Flume quickly became the most popular ride at the park, and was soon imitated around the world. It has since gone through numerous permutations, from the "whitewater rivers" of the 1980s, which used circular rafts, fake rocks, waterfalls, and rapids to suggest a ride on a real river, to the "extreme water rides" of the 1990s, which are a cross between roller coasters and traditional flumes.

But no matter what the packaging, the reason for the popularity of these rides has always remained the same: Everyone loves to get drenched with water on a hot summer day. But this begs a further question, at least in the mind of the suspicious and easily distracted: Where does the log ride get its water?

The simple—and disconcerting—answer: From the sewer. Most log rides are attached to the common water system for the area, also known as the local sewer. Once pumped, the water is cycled continuously through the Flume, with a stop at a chlorinated filter each round. The only water lost to the system is the slop over the edges and the moisture you carry away in your soaking-wet clothes.

While water standards vary from state to state, most log rides must legally maintain the same cleanliness level as a public pool. In other words, don't drink the water—you know what little kids do in those pools. Fortunately, log rides are inspected by the government for floating objects on a regular basis.

The only other standard is that the water in the ride must be clear enough to see if someone is drowning in it. This is a real safety rule in almost all states that bother with rules in the first place, and one you'll no doubt agree seems quite practical and thoughtful.

In general, outside the tiny danger of drowning in its one foot of clear water, the classic flume is mind-numbingly safe. The ride is, after all, a slow glide toward one nice big splash. If the splash doesn't live up to the hype—which, unfortunately, it rarely does—the whole thing can be a pretty boring experience.

So what's a ride-junkie to do? The answer is simple: Put the heaviest people in the front of the log, which will create a bigger splash. Many parks try to prevent this seating arrangement (they secretly hate the big splash), which is too bad because putting large people in front isn't dangerous, and it's way more fun.

So go ahead and put the big man in the lead seat. This is one situation where it's well worth it to break the rules.

# Over The Edge . . .

On Saturday, May 28, 1984, three teenagers were strapped into the newest ride sensation at Six Flags Great America in Gurnee, Illinois, The Edge. The ride lifted you up a thin metal shaft several hundred feet into the air, shifted you out over the edge of the tower, then let you "fall" straight down along two vertical rails.

Unfortunately, just as the teenagers' car neared the top of the tower, the lift mechanism broke. The car plummeted back down the shaft, crashing at the bottom with such force that the seats curled up around the victims. All three teenagers were wearing "I Went Over The Edge . . . And Survived" T-shirts at the time. Although seriously injured, all three young men survived (proving once again that t-shirts don't lie).

The ride, a new variety developed in Switzerland known as a "freefall," had been designed without a brake in the tower. Subsequent designs incorporated this safety device, and freefalls are now one of the most popular and safest rides in American amusement parks.

But it was too late for The Edge. The ride was dismantled by Great America and sold to the Rocky Point Amusement Park in Warwick, Maine. When that park went out of business, the ride moved to a park in Oklahoma, then on to a park in Ohio where it now operates, modified with a safety break, under the name "Mr. Hyde's Nasty Fall."

# The Vomitorium

In stick-to-the-wall rides, the centrifugal force of the spinning room pins you to the wall. When the floor drops away, you are suspended in midair against the wall.

There are a lot of names for this ride, including the futuristic-themed Gravitron 2100 (also commonly known as Starship 2100), which used to be the Gravitron 2000 until the turn of the millennium forced carnies to change the zero to a one. After all, no one wants a "futuristic" ride named after a year that's already past. Another common name is the Hell Hole, which features paintings and cutouts of demons and other fiery minions.

No matter the theme, all these rides have a common nickname around the carnival: The vomitorium. Sniff closely upon

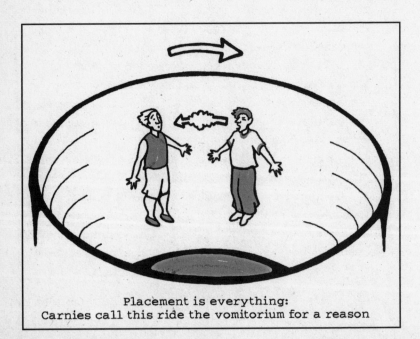

Placement is everything:
Carnies call this ride the vomitorium for a reason

entering, and you're almost sure to detect the slight undertone of puke beneath the smell of sweat and antiseptic. If you've spent any time around the carnival at all, you probably know someone who's puked on this ride. It's kind of a rite of passage among the weak of stomach.

Indeed, if there's one ride that is sure to make your friend, rival, or casual acquaintance upchuck on his shorts, it's a stick-to-the-wall ride. If your friend has just eaten a corn dog, sausage, or other heavy carnival food, it's almost a guarantee. Obviously, it's practically your duty to sucker them into making this mistake.

If you're going to play this joke, however, you must remember one thing: Choose your position carefully. If the ride is revolving to the right, and you are riding on the victim's left, the joke—and the vomit—is going to be on you.

# Beware the Clown Head

In March 2001, the unthinkable happened: A giant inflatable clown head turned deadly.

The incident occurred at a local carnival in a small town in Australia. Several children were playing inside the inflatable clown head (which was really just an interestingly shaped Moon Bounce) when a sudden gust of wind caused the head to break free from its moorings and fly about 10 feet into the air.

Twelve people were injured, including eleven children. Five of the children were hospitalized with serious injuries. An eight-year-old girl died of massive head trauma.

While experts have long predicted such a catastrophe—inflatable rides run neck and neck with carousels as the most dangerous amusement attraction for young children—the incident still shakes a person's faith.

A killer inflatable clown head: Is nothing safe or sacred?

# *Romance on the Rides*

A certain logic says a roller coaster is a great place to make a move on your date. It goes like this: Roller coasters are scary, there's a lot of jostling and arms waving in the air, so it's the perfect time to slip your arm "accidentally" around your date and "reassure" him (or her) that everything is A-OK.

This logic is flawed. A coaster is wild—too wild. No matter how smooth your moves, your date is much more likely to get an elbow to the mouth than the kiss you were going for.

For romance, your best opportunity is a slow, dark ride. Haunted houses and tunnels of love are practically built for making out, but any ride where you float on a lazy channel of water while animatronic figures sing, dance, and swig fake moonshine will do. Besides, the scenery is usually so painfully hokey you need to find something more interesting to occupy your time.

If you're planning to make a move, always ride in the back of the car. It is nearly impossible to get romantic with strangers—or even worse, your friends—looking over your shoulder. And don't worry about the workers: Carnies know these rides are made for love. At Epcot Center's Spaceship Earth, a favorite make-out ride because it's leisurely, air-conditioned, and entirely private when you're going up or down the hills, the employees have a saying: "Front seat for the view, backseat for the hanky-panky."

Ferris wheels are also highly recommended for a make-out session. The air is refreshingly odor-free at that altitude, and the view is often magnificent: Cattle lowing in the 4-H barn, haystacks casting evening shadows, the long line of taillights on the cars leaving the fair . . . what could be more romantic?

Besides, the Ferris wheel is notoriously boring; without a little interpersonal action you might find yourself falling asleep up there.

Many people have reported getting busy in the skybuckets, but few report having enjoyed it.

In short, any ride above the sightlines of prying eyes is a safe place for a little action. Just be careful: Don't ever unlock a seat belt or hang over the edge. Expressing your affection is a noble pursuit, but it's not worth your life.

If someone suggests you come along on one of these rides, suspect the inevitable. If you ask someone to accompany you, realize that they probably suspect your intentions. In either case, take a lesson from the Boy Scouts and be prepared. As the saying goes, you don't want to be caught with your pants down.

# Coaster Park U.S.A.

There are two types of amusement parks: So-called family parks like Disney World and thrill parks. Disney is fine for small children, pasty computer geeks, and canoodling couples, but for flat-out fun and excitement, you can't beat a good coaster park.

There are currently 658 roller coasters (and counting) in America. While that may seem like a lot—it would take you almost two solid years of riding every day to test them all—it's less than half the 1,400 coasters operating at the height of the amusement park craze in the 1920s. But don't pine for the past. Two of America's great coaster parks hail from that golden age: Cedar Point in Sandusky, Ohio, and Kennywood in western Pennsylvania.

Cedar Point, founded in 1870, decided long ago to differentiate itself from the crowd by concentrating almost exclusively on roller coasters. The park features fourteen of them, representing almost every era of coaster design—more coasters than in any amusement park in the world until Six Flags Magic Mountain passed it in 2002. With that many coasters, there are bound to be some duds, but Cedar Point can be

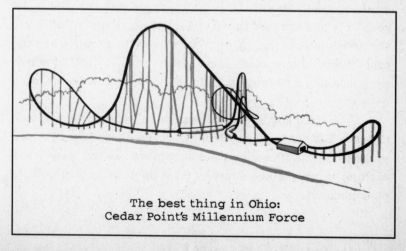

The best thing in Ohio:
Cedar Point's Millennium Force

forgiven for flops like Gemini (see "Field Guide to Roller Coasters") because it has one true stud: Millennium Force, one of the few coasters in the world to top 300 feet.

Kennywood, meanwhile, is most famous for its pleasant tree-shaded walks and two 1920s-era wooden masterpieces: Jack Rabbit (1921) and The Racer (1927), both designed by America's first coaster genius, John Miller. But this park has never rested on its past accomplishments, as proven by its three heart-rattling modern-era coasters, including the legendary Thunderbolt, which drops dramatically into a natural ravine (an adaptation of a 1924 John Miller design). In 1987, Kennywood became the first amusement park listed on the National Register of Historic Places, an appropriate honor for one of America's premier roller-coaster meccas.

The true titan of the thrill-park world, however, is corporate honcho Six Flags. The chain is named for the six countries that at one time or another have claimed the great State of Texas, the site of its first park, which opened outside Dallas in 1961. The company owns and operates 39 amusement parks, including 30 in North America.

While Disney has always been about family, Six Flags has always been all about wickedly fun rides. The company isn't afraid to push the envelope. Six Flags created the first roller coaster where the cars travel under the rail (Batman the Ride), the first coaster to top 100 mph (Superman the Escape), and the first "fourth-dimension" roller coaster (X), a freewheeling, somersaulting extravaganza that has to be experienced to be believed.

The company is also known for its eagerness to snatch the cash. Batman the Ride, for instance, was exactly reproduced to the same specifications at six separate locations. Now that's cashing in on market share—and a short-term pop culture phenomenon!

# Roller Coaster Science

So what is a roller coaster anyway? The answer can be found not only in the name of the ride, but in the title of the first coaster in the world: LaMarcus Thompson's Switchback Gravity Pleasure Railway, which opened at Coney Island, Brooklyn, in 1884.

No, the key word isn't railway, it's *gravity*. Roller coasters are, by definition, rides that use gravity to propel a train of rolling cars down a track. In other words, they are rollers that coast. True roller coasters don't have an engine, either in the track or on the cars. Instead, they have a lift system to raise the cars to the top of a big hill. The momentum gained from dropping down the steep side of that hill propels the cars through the rest of the ride.

**The Third Wheel.** The modern coaster era began in 1912, when John Miller patented his design for the underfriction roller coaster car. The breakthrough was a third set of wheels that wraps under the track and holds the car against the rails. This eliminates the jostling and banging of earlier designs (which ate up a lot of momentum) and reduces drag. Underfriction allowed coasters to be taller, steeper, and faster than anything previously imagined.

**The Woodie.** Miller built hundreds of underfriction roller coasters out of the only materials available at the time, solid metal tracks on wood. Wood is heavy and will snap if the individual boards are too long, so it needs an intricate system of bracing. This limits the maximum height of the ride to less than 200 feet. Since the momentum of the coaster is based entirely on gravity, and gravity has more of an effect the higher you get, this also limits the speed. Because of these shortcomings, wooden coasters went out of style when a new alternative arose.

John Miller's breakthrough 1912 wheel
design, still in use today

Between 1960 and 1980, most of the wooden coasters in America were torn down in favor of steel.

**Totally Tubular.** The second revolution in roller coaster science took place in 1959 with the completion of Disneyland's Matterhorn, the first steel roller coaster. Tubular (hollow) steel is so light and strong that it needs very little bracing or support. The Matterhorn proved steel was a viable alternative to wood, and roller coasters instantly started a race to be higher and steeper than the competition, which soon doubled the average ride speed.

The strength and durability of steel also granted designers the opportunity to create new shapes and styles. The first helix (corkscrew) was introduced at Knott's Berry Farm in 1963. The first upside down loop debuted at Six Flags Magic Mountain in 1975. The first inverted train was unveiled by the Six Flags Corporation in 1992. Its success resulted in an explosion of new seating configurations, including stand-up, inverted, and flying (lying down beneath the track) coasters. There are now coasters where riders face backwards, floorless coasters, and even coasters where riders hang off the car on a rotating pole (see X, in "A Field Guide to Roller Coasters"). But through it all, two things remained constant: The exclusive use of gravity and the underfriction design system patented by John Miller in 1912.

**The Return of the Woodie.** Starting in the 1970s, wooden roller coasters began to make a comeback, typified by the triumphant 1979 unveiling of Beast at King's Island in Ohio. They may be shorter and slower than their steel competition, but woodies offer one thing steel never can: Sway. Unlike metal, wood bends under heavy weight, so a wooden coaster rocks and drops as the train passes over it. Designers built new wooden coasters to maximize this flex, and serious coaster enthusiasts claim they can feel the difference in the structure from ride to ride.

Wood also adds a psychological thrill. It creaks in the wind. Boards break. The paint chips off and the chain drive clicks loudly as the train is pulled up the first hill. This is all part of the drama. A good coaster crew keeps a wooden coaster looking and sounding shoddy to enhance the thrill. Don't worry—unless you're at a tenth-rate park (and only you know if you're that cheap), that coaster decay is purely cosmetic. The Cyclone at Coney Island is a perfect example of the decrepit-is-scary-and-fun philosophy of wooden coaster maintenance.

**Motor Mania.** Since the 1970s, there has been another revolution in coaster science: The use of linear motors, lasers, and computers to propel the cars along the track. The breakthrough in motors came in 1997, when Magic Mountain's Superman the Escape used motors to exceed 100 mph for the first time. The cost, however, was heavy: Superman took the coast entirely out of the coaster.

Are motors the wave of the future? Maybe . . . and maybe not. New technology is not always a step forward, and coaster designers have been wrong before. In the 1980s, for instance, the hot new design was upside-down loops. Many parks built shuttle coasters in which you simply go forward through a gigantic loop, then backwards through the same loop to the starting point. Riders soon realized that the thrills were short, and the aftermath, like headaches and dizziness, weren't worth the effort of standing in line. Today, most shuttle-loop coasters have been dismantled or are sitting idle.

Are motorized cars the shuttle loop of the new millennium? Only time—and rider trauma—will tell.

# G-Force and the
# Brain Scrambler

With the added height and shapes made possible by steel comes an extra element of danger. It's not the speed, or the verticality of the drop, or the sideways flip that convinces you your glasses are going to fall off. It's the combination of all three, which create an effect known as g-forces.

G-forces are a measure of gravity, or pressure. They are caused by high speeds and tight turns or, even worse, both at once. Roller coasters are one of the few places where an ordinary citizen can experience high g's, which occur mostly on loops, corkscrews, and at the bottom of hills that are higher than 300 feet.

Many consider high g's the ultimate coaster thrill; others consider them a disaster waiting to happen. Germany has outlawed any coaster that causes the rider to experience more than 4.5 g's (almost five times the normal force of gravity). Most of the newest and fastest American coasters routinely surpass this limit.

High g-forces have been known to make riders get dizzy, see spots, have brown-outs in their vision, or momentarily lose consciousness. After all, they are the same forces that sometimes cause fighter-jet pilots to black out during maneuvers. The physical symptoms are the result of a lack of blood to the brain: The pressure from the g-force is so high that the heart simply can't pump hard enough to move the blood through the veins.

Since high g-forces on most coasters last about a second, the effects are temporary and harmless . . . unless you have a preexisting brain or heart condition, like the weakened blood vessel known as an aneurysm. After all, a few seconds without blood to the brain is nothing to a healthy human. But how do you know you're healthy until it's too late?

Far worse for the average rider are helixes and corkscrews that thrash your head from side to side. This whiplash motion can cause neck and back injuries, not to mention a sloshing of the brain. Some rides have head restraints to counter this problem, but most serious coaster enthusiasts don't like them. The restraints don't fit all riders tightly, so 90 percent still get their heads thrashed around during the ride, with the extra thrill of their whiplashed head richocheting off the sides of the restraint.

Despite rumors to the contrary, head injuries are not funny, especially when they happen to you. If you experience nausea, vomiting, or dizziness after exiting a roller coaster, see a doctor.

# Killer Coasters

It's one thing for a ride to kill when it is not maintained properly or when the victim does something stupid, like unbuckle his seat belt, stand up, or go into a restricted area under the coaster to retrieve his hat (a decision that killed a man in 1988 under Six Flags Great America's Top Gun). It's another thing entirely when someone dies or is seriously injured during the course of a normal coaster ride.

The following accidents are not listed here because they are especially terrifying or gruesome. They are simply a selection of recent injuries that have occurred at major American theme parks.

For the most part, these serious injuries and deaths were the result of undetected medical conditions. It is important to remember that no one has ever conclusively proven that coasters in working condition kill healthy human beings. In fact, a scientific study sponsored by Six Flags recently "proved" that roller coasters are safer than taking a warm shower (an act that kills hundreds every year).

This list in no way, shape, or form is meant to imply that you should avoid these thrill rides (unless you have a medical condition, of course). In fact, exactly the opposite is true. You are strongly encouraged to ride all of the following coasters. Not only are they some of the best rides in America, the "killer coaster" image gives them an extra thrill factor you just can't get on the local Ferris wheel.

- **Perilous Plunge, Knott's Berry Farm (2001).** A 292-pound woman was ejected from her seat on this "extreme water coaster" (a cross between a log ride and a roller coaster) as it went over the final 115-foot drop. She died from multiple blunt trauma. It is suspected her size was a contributing factor in the accident.

- **Montezooma's Revenge, Knott's Berry Farm (2001).** Only three weeks before the Perilous Plunge incident, a more traditional coaster at Knott's Berry Farm turned killer. In this instance, the twenty-five-year-old female victim collapsed during the ride and died. She had suffered a fatal brain hemorrhage related to a preexisting condition.

- **Monkey Business, Six Flags Marine World (2001).** After riding twice, a woman complained of a headache and numbness on her left side. She was treated by park EMT and then transferred to the hospital, where she died two days later of a brain hemorrhage. Amazingly, Monkey Business isn't even a roller coaster—it's a spinning ride, like the Mad Hatter's Tea Cups at Disney World.

- **Goliath, Six Flags Magic Mountain (2001).** A woman was found dead in her seat when this monster coaster pulled into the station. She had suffered a fatal brain hemorrhage, the first death in what would turn out to be a killer summer for the amusement park industry.

- **Indiana Jones Adventure, Disneyland (2000).** A twenty-three-year-old woman complained of a headache after exiting the ride. She returned to her hotel, where she passed out. She never regained consciousness and died two months later of complications from a brain hemorrhage. This was not the first incident involving Dr. Jones. In 1998, a middle-aged woman suffered a brain hemorrhage, resulting in long-term disabilities. Disney paid her an undisclosed settlement. In the late 1980s, another woman began projectile vomiting after exiting the ride and within hours fell into a coma. She underwent three emergency surgeries, but was left with permanent brain damage.

- **Steel Force, Dorney Park (1997).** A woman began suffering headaches soon after riding this 300-foot-high coaster. A neurologist discovered a spinal-fluid leak caused by a tear in the lining of her brain, but only circumstantial evidence could ever link the tear to the coaster.

# Backseat Action

It's a fact: The seat you choose on the roller coaster matters. Because of high-science concepts like g-forces, inertia, and momentum, every single seat in the train of every single roller coaster presents you with a unique and different ride.

That's not to say that most of the yahoos lining up for the front car aren't just that—yahoos. The first car gives you a great view, especially of the track on those big drops, but it's not the car the experts choose. For the ride of your life, always ride in the back.

The secret to a great roller coaster isn't the loops—it's the speed. The best thrill on most coasters is the first big drop. Now think about this: When the first car is 50 feet down the drop, the back car is still just topping the hill. In other words, the front car has to drag the rest of the train over the hill, making it the slowest car in the train. By the time the back car reaches the top of the hill, the rest of the cars are already pulling it forward at high speed.

The result is not just a faster ride, but greater lift. In the backseat, the sling-shot effect caused by the downward pull of the other cars will actually lift the rider a few inches out of his or her seat at the top of some hills. In fact, most coasters are designed with small hills whose entire purpose is to achieve this effect. This lift—known as negative g's or airtime—is the holy grail of coaster riding.

If the thought of achieving airtime makes you queasy, choose a car in the center of the train toward the front. These are often referred to as "wimp cars," but as long as the coaster isn't a dud they still provide a great ride.

For maximum thrill, make sure the attendant doesn't lock the lap bar or floor restraint too far down on your waist or legs.

When they come by, thrust your hips forward and cheat your legs up by rising onto your tiptoes. This gives you a little room to move around, which will result in a few seconds of extra airtime. Don't worry: Those pesky g-forces don't pose any real danger as long as you're sitting down.

Last but not least, don't be a stickler for the Backseat Rule. It's not always worth waiting extra rides for this favored car. The second to the rearmost seat is practically as good, so climb aboard and start screaming your lungs out.

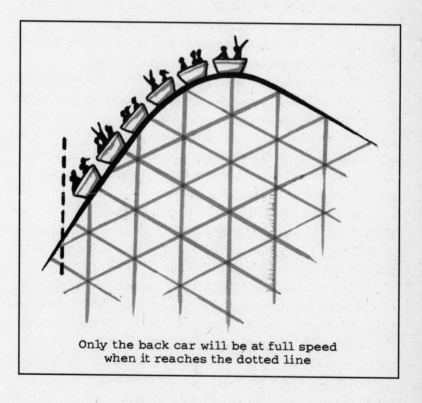

Only the back car will be at full speed
when it reaches the dotted line

# The Front Seat Exception

There are exceptions to the Backseat Rule. On some rides, you're better off in the front seat, where you get the thrill of seeing the track racing in front of you and a view unimpeded by waving hands and flying hair.

Besides, people who don't know much about coasters think riding in the front car is the ultimate in macho. So throw your hands up and yell like a demon: You might as well get cool points while you can, because they don't come free.

The most common exception to the Backseat Rule is the slow coaster. These rides don't go fast enough to give you the lift or the tight turns that real coaster nuts crave. Space Mountain is the classic example. Despite the hype, Space Mountain is little more than a kiddie coaster with the lights out. You'll get the best ride in the first seat . . . if you can get it.

The other exception is a really old coaster, like the Cyclone at Coney Island. The Cyclone isn't the oldest roller coaster in the world, but it was the first to symbolize the thrill (and danger) of the Midway in the public mind. It is a coaster to be admired and praised, but not ridden in the back car.

The back car on the Cyclone is like spending four minutes in a blender. The ride is old and creaky (it's rumored that the nails must be pounded back into place every morning), causing the train to jump along the tracks instead of coast. As the train jumps, riders in the back are thrown violently from side to side, whacking their knees and elbows on the sides of the tiny car and snapping their neck and spine back and forth.

If you don't believe the seat you choose makes a difference, take two rides on the Cyclone. Ride the front car first, because you'll have such a good time you'll want to ride more. Now try the back car: You'll be walking crooked for a week.

An ornery old man (but still the king)

# A Field Guide to Roller Coasters

Does anybody care about the best bumper cars in America? How about the best Tilt-a-Whirl or circular swings? Even a discussion of water rides, which can be very different from one another, gets boring as soon as the topic of wet T-shirts is exhausted. There are those that will argue about Ferris wheels and merry-go-rounds, but the obvious truth must be stated here: Those guys are nerds.

Meanwhile, thousands of people debate the merits of roller coasters every day. Tales are swapped of truly excellent or disappointing rides. Top Ten coaster lists are as common as unflattering khaki shorts on middle-aged men, and entire television programs are dedicated to the bizarre opinions of goggle-eyed coaster fanatics.

Which doesn't necessarily help you choose the best park to visit, or the line worth waiting in once you're there. This list, however, should do just that.

# Fastest, Tallest, Longest Drop:
## Superman the Escape

**Location:** Six Flags Magic Mountain, Valencia, CA

**Manufacturer:** Intamin AG

**Year:** 1997

**Height:** 415 feet

**Drop:** 328 feet

**Maximum Speed:** 100 mph

**Length:** 1,315 feet (twice)

**Outstanding Feature:** An adrenaline junky's dream . . . for about 7 seconds

Superman is supersized. It's 100 feet taller than the nearest competition. It drops 30 stories. And it was the first coaster to reach 100 mph (although Dodonpa at Fuji-Q Highlands in Japan now tops it at 106.9 mph). In the race for the biggest and the baddest, it gives all others a wedgie and leaves them hanging from a peg in the locker room.

The ride blasts you from 0 to 100 mph in 7 seconds, with an outrageous 6.5 seconds of airtime. Then you do the same thing in reverse.

Then it's over. Wait . . . this ride has massive speed, drop, and airtime—but there's just no drama.

# Fastest, Tallest, Longest Drop Honorable Mention:
## Millennium Force

**Location:** Cedar Point, Sandusky, OH

**Manufacturer:** Intamin AG

**Year:** 2000

**Height:** 310 feet

**Drop:** 300 feet

**Length:** 6,595 feet

**Maximum Speed:** 93 mph

**Outstanding Feature:** The 80-degree drop off a massive hill is like skydiving without a parachute

Purists don't consider Superman a coaster since there's no coast: It's all driven by a motor. That leaves all honors to Millennium Force. The drop here is incredibly steep, and at 310 feet it's higher than the Statue of Liberty or 7,400 cans of Pepsi stacked on top of each other. Wow.

Millennium Force has tiered seating, which is nice since the view out over the Great Lakes is lovely—especially when you know the inevitable fall is coming. Almost as good as the drop are the overbanked turns, which are as close as you can get to an inversion without going all the way over.

# Longest Coaster:
## Beast

---

**Location:** Paramount King's Island, Cincinnati, OH

**Manufacturer:** Dinn Corp.

**Year:** 1979

**Height:** 135 feet

**Drop:** 141 feet (second lift)

**Length:** 7,400 feet

**Maximum Speed:** 64.8 mph

**Outstanding Feature:** The beautiful woodland setting makes this one of the few great coasters that should be ridden up front—after a trip in the back, of course

---

Beast isn't the fastest coaster around, and it doesn't have a huge drop or massive air, but it may be the best-designed coaster in America. It gives everything a coaster can give: Drops, air, twists, a fabulous tunnel, and a very, very long ride that never gets repetitive or boring. That's why, despite the fact that it's an old man at more than twenty years, it continues to make most best coaster lists.

# Best Wooden Coaster:
## Ghost Rider

**Location:** Knott's Berry Farm, Buena Park, CA

**Manufacturer:** Custom Coasters International

**Year:** 1998

**Height:** 118 feet

**Drop:** 108 feet

**Length:** 4,533 feet

**Maximum Speed:** 56 mph

**Outstanding Feature:** The twisting, serpentine course makes you feel totally out of control—and puts the break in breakneck

This retro-wooden coaster is basically Coney Island's Cyclone on steroids. It has the same basic layout, with more of everything. This ride is fast and furious, with a wicked bank off every hill, including an ingenious twist off the first drop. The tilt keeps you off balance, and the ride never gives you a second to breathe—you're always reacting. And, like all classic wooden coasters, Ghost Rider provides massive airtime.

# Best Steel Coaster:
## Steel Force

**Location:** Dorney Park, Allentown, PA

**Manufacturer:** D. H. Morgan

**Year:** 1997

**Height:** 300 feet

**Drop:** 205 feet

**Length:** 5,600 feet

**Maximum Speed:** 75 mph

**Outstanding Feature:** The most terrifying hill in America is only the beginning

If the key to a great ride is speed, drop, and airtime, Steel Force wins the Triple Crown. This is a huge coaster with a thin, almost flimsy-looking frame that towers over the rest of the park. It's all part of the effect. Steel Force blasts out of a massive first drop, then throttles you through a thrill-filled ride. The four "camelback" hills near the end provide some of the best airtime in North America. Not the longest ride in the world, but it packs a punch like a prizefighter.

# Most Disappointing Coaster:
## Gemini

**Location:** Cedar Point, Sandusky, OH

**Manufacturer:** Arrow Dynamics

**Year:** 1975

**Height:** 125 feet

**Drop:** 118 feet

**Length:** 3,935 feet

**Maximum Speed:** 60 mph

**Outstanding Feature:** You get to watch the riders in the parallel train to see if they're as bored as you are

Gemini proves that, yes, 7.5 million riders can be wrong. This 1970s clunker, which features the gimmick of two parallel trains, misses all the marks: No drop, no airtime, and oh so painfully slow. Gemini is more like taking a scenic tour on a corkscrew than riding a roller coaster. You get just as many thrills on the junior version they made for the kids.

# Oldest Coaster:
## Leap-the-Dips

**Location:** Lakemont Park, Allentown, PA

**Manufacturer:** E. Joy Morris Company

**Year:** 1902

**Height:** 41 feet

**Drop:** 9 feet

**Length:** 1,452 feet

**Maximum Speed:** 10 mph

**Outstanding Feature:** Man, this coaster is really, really old

With a top speed of 10 mph and a drop of only 9 feet, Leap-the-Dips isn't exactly cutting edge. In fact, it's the last known example of a side-friction figure-eight roller coaster, a design that went extinct in 1912 when everyone realized the physics stink. But give Leap-the-Dips credit: It has stood on the same site for more than one hundred years and, in 1996, was designated a National Historic Landmark. Top that, Superman the Escape!

# The Coaster of the Future:
## X

**Location:** Six Flags Magic Mountain, Valencia, CA

**Manufacturer:** Arrow Dynamics

**Year:** 2002

**Height:** 290 feet

**Drop:** 215 feet

**Top Speed:** 76 mph

**Length:** 3,610 feet

**Outstanding Feature:** A 200-foot drop, suspended in the air, facing straight down at the ground: You will laugh and cry at the exact same time

X is so Xtreme that they had to create a new type of coaster designation: Fourth dimension. The track is typical; the cars are anything but. While the empty "car" rides the rails, the riders are suspended from seats on 10-foot poles dangling off the side, so far from the track they can't even see it. Not enough for you? The poles spin, pivoting you in all different directions— straight up, on your stomach, upside down—even as the track takes you over massive hills and through a full loop. Now that's Xstasy in the Xtreme.

If you don't think science is cool, take a ride on X. Is that the future you're feeling? It better be.

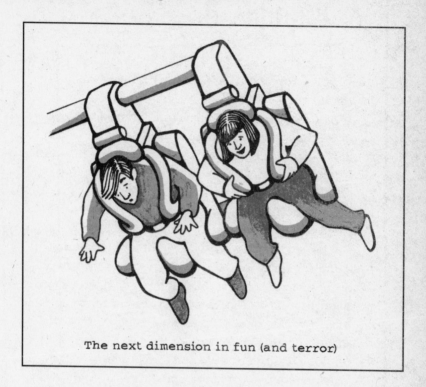

The next dimension in fun (and terror)

# A Pretty Boy Gets His

One of the most bizarre, and hilarious, accidents in carnival history took place in May 1999 in Williamsburg, Virginia.

Busch Gardens Williamsburg, one of the most popular theme parks in the country, was debuting a new roller coaster called Apollo's Chariot. For the inaugural ride, the park enlisted the services of C-list celebrity Fabio, a male model best known for his appearances on romance novel covers and in "I Can't Believe It's Not Butter" television commercials.

Before the ride began, the horse-faced hunk was playing up his resemblance to the manly god Apollo, strutting for the cameras and laughing it up with a roller coaster full of beautiful women wearing faux-Grecian tunics. By the end of the ride, Fabio was bloody, disoriented, and headed for the hospital.

What caused this twisted turn of events? It seems that, against all odds, sometime during the ride Fabio had been hit directly in the face by a low-flying bird.

Fabio survived with only minor cuts and bruises. The bird (reportedly a goose, although the perpetrator was never publicly identified) was not so lucky. Its broken, lifeless body was fished out of a nearby body of water a few hours after the incident.

The bird's motive has never been definitely ascertained.

# Rocket Rods: Disney's Big Dud

Making speed rides fun is difficult. Building them is even harder. Physics is a tricky wicket, and no matter how many tests you run, the chance for failure (and embarrassment) is always right around the corner. Just ask our friends at Disney.

The Disney corporate honchos realized long ago they needed to spruce up Disneyland's sparsely populated and decidedly old-school Tomorrowland. They came up with the idea for Rocket Rods, individual cars that looked like hot rods and could blast around a track at up to 65 miles per hour. The ride would be another breakthrough for the trailblazing park: The first speed ride to feature a separate engine in each car.

Rumors about Rocket Rods swirled among amusement park aficionados and Disney maniacs for almost a decade. The advertising campaign kicked off a year before the ride was scheduled to open, touting the speed and technical innovation that would blast Tomorrowland back to the future (despite the fact that the theme was decidedly nouveau-1950s). Disney unveiled their newest masterpiece in 1998 and waited for the accolades to pour in.

But there had been a serious miscalculation. In order to increase efficiency and keep costs down, Disney imagineers had decided that, instead of building a new track for the ride, they would simply use the old People Mover track. But the People Mover used a flat track. Without banked curves, the rocket rods couldn't safely reach their maximum speeds. Their fastest safe speed was only 35 miles per hour, which turned a ride based on velocity into something about as fun as riding in your mom's minivan.

Almost immediately after opening, Rocket Rods was shut down for repairs. The old People Mover track wasn't just slow, it was also shredding tires. The ride reopened, but the repairs didn't take. The ride was shut down several more times over the ensuing months, before being shelved for good before its first birthday. Despite the hype of a yearlong advertising campaign, the cost of Rocket Rods repairs was simply too much for the Mouse to bear.

# 5

# FREAKS AND GEEKS:
# SIDESHOWS REVEALED

The sideshow has been
called many things:
Brilliant, bizarre,
disgusting, scary,
exploitative, and sexy.
Many people think the
sideshow is dead, and
they are happy about its
passing.

They're fools. The sideshow is a
grand tradition, an art form, an
important part of our cultural
heritage. Fortunately, there are
still a few freaks (in the best
sense of the word) toiling to keep
this lost world alive.

# The 10-in-1

The classic sideshow is the 10-in-1: A menagerie that offers ten acts for one admission price. The acts are traditionally a mix of skilled performers like a sword swallower, and biological freaks like the Walrus Man and Alligator Girl.

The key to the show is the inside talker. Also known as the Lecturer or the Professor, the inside talker is the freak-a-thon emcee. The 10-in-1 is a continuous loop with no intermission, usually taking about 30 minutes, and it's the Professor's job to keep the audience properly focused and the action in high gear. If dead spots arise—for instance, if the fire breather is arguing with his snake-handling girlfriend backstage—the inside talker is always ready with some quick banter or, even better, magic tricks and illusions to keep the show's momentum moving forward.

The inside talker, like most sideshow performers, is usually a master of many skills. He may be a magician first and foremost, but he will also be able to perform Human Blockhead, fire-breathing, bed of nails, sword swallowing, electric chair, and other classic acts. In some old traveling sideshows, the inside talker performed four or five of the ten acts himself, especially if another performer was sick, drunk, injured, or in any other way unable to perform.

Most sideshow artists and inside talkers have "non-freak" skills as well, such as carpenter, electrician, or banner painter. Unless the show is famous, the performers are usually responsible for building the set at each stop, and for keeping the equipment in working order.

The golden age of the sideshow is long past. Sideshows by the Seashore, located on New York City's Coney Island (and commonly referred to as the Coney Island Freak Show), is the last 10-in-1 in America featuring all the classic acts, although these rarely feature actual deformed human beings.

This is not because of political correctness or a lack of trying. Thanks to advances in medicine and more opportunities for the handicapped, biological freaks looking for sideshow work are now few and far between. Dwarfs and giants are the most common modern freaks, especially together as an odd-couple act. The tattooed man (or woman) is still an industry staple, despite the fact that everyone from rock stars to bikers has copied this style of hardcore body art. One of the last bearded ladies left the business in the late 1990s. An outspoken feminist, she went on to found her own successful circus and to lecture at UCLA.

While the fall of the freak is unfortunate, there is one classic sideshow stunt that no one in his right mind should mourn: The geek act, which was shelved in the 1960s not because of good taste on the part of spectators but because of health regulations and animal rights protests.

A geek show involves biting the head off a live animal onstage, usually a chicken, although any medium-sized animal (including Ozzy's bat) will serve in a pinch. Clearly, this act involves no skill, but merely a freakish willingness to do something grotesque and unhealthy for pretty lousy pay. This is why, in the sideshow as in most modern middle schools, the lowest of the low is to be a geek.

# Freaks

Freaks, in the carnival sense of the word, are people paid to display their physical deformities. They were traditionally part of a 10-in-1 or, if famous or spectacular enough, performed alongside a sideshow or carnival as a separate attraction with a separate admission, called a single-o.

Most people assume freaks fell out of favor because the act is exploitative. This is untrue. Freak shows gave otherwise hopeless human beings a chance to be productive citizens, especially in a less enlightened era, and provided a family-like environment of like-minded people.

This is not to say life as a sideshow freak was easy. After all, these performers were paid to be gawked at, poked, prodded, and often despised. Unfortunately, life in the outside world would have been much the same, and they wouldn't have received a penny for the injustice.

For the most part, freak shows were and are honest entertainment. The most common gaffs include wrinkled hags claiming to be preposterously old and storytellers lying about their participation in famous events or their friendships with famous dead folk. If the act relies on being told something incredible about the freak without visible verification, don't believe the hype.

Honest-to-goodness freak acts like Walrus Man, Dog-Faced Boy, Sealo, and Siamese Twins were the driving force behind the sideshow for years. As with all things carnival, the brilliance (and the money) was often in the setup. Giants stood beside midgets and sold huge rings as souvenirs. Fat men and bearded ladies appeared as couples, even if they weren't together outside the show. Deformed performers like the original Walrus Man, who had stubs for arms and propelled his huge body along the ground with flipperlike feet, performed in cages.

Occasionally, they would rush at the audience or bark in order to seem more frightening and strange.

These acts were immensely popular around the turn of the century. Famous freaks toured nationally, with huge advertising budgets and elaborate tents, and were often invited to meet royalty, politicians, and celebrities. General Tom Thumb, an anatomically normal man who topped out at just three feet four inches tall, grossed more than two million dollars in less than three years on tour—at 25 cents per admission! He lived in an enormous mansion and is rumored to have bailed his old boss P. T. Barnum out of financial ruin later in his life.

Now who was exploiting whom?

# Classic Freak Acts

Over the years, freak shows realized that a handful of diseases produced the most popular human attractions. Some of the diseases, like phocomelia (Seal Boy), occur only once in several hundred thousand births. Others are fairly common and harmless—the skin condition icthyosis (Alligator Man), for instance, strikes one in every 250 Americans. In all cases, sideshows freaks exhibited extreme versions of the condition that were truly one in a million.

**Albino.** The performer has pink eyes and lacks all pigment in his skin and hair, making him stark white. Negro albinos were particularly popular in early sideshows.

**Alligator Man.** A person afflicted with a condition, usually icthyosis, that makes the skin scaly and reptilian. A variation is the Elephant Skin Man or Rubber-Skinned Woman, performers whose skin is extremely baggy and loose.

**Frog Man.** A performer who can squat in a froglike position with his knees behind his back, usually the result of the hyperextensive joints and rubbery skin common to Ehlers-Danlos syndrome.

**Half Girl.** A person born without legs. A performer born without arms or legs was known as the Human Torso.

**Human Cigarette Factory.** The Human Cigarette Factory was the legendary Otis Jordan, a paraplegic who had to be strapped to an upright support and wheeled onstage. Once there, he would pick up a cigarette paper, roll a cigarette, pick up a matchbook, strike a match, light the cigarette, douse the match, and take a few puffs—all using only his mouth. The most amazing fact about this act: Otis Jordan didn't smoke!

**Lobster Boy.** A person with an inherited birth defect that causes his hands to fuse into claws, starting at the wrist. The disease also commonly strikes the feet of its victims.

**Monkey Girl.** An extreme form of the bearded lady, these performers had hair all over their body. Alternate names include Wolf Boy and Dog Girl.

**Pinhead.** An individual with an extreme case of microcephaly, a condition that causes the head to be smaller than normal and come to a point.

**Seal Boy/Penguin Boy.** A performer with phocomelia, which causes very short limbs or, in some extreme cases, causes the hands and feet to grow directly from the torso.

Mignon the Penguin Girl performed on a block of ice in the 1950s

# Freaks of the Animal Kingdom

Animal freaks, like human freaks, are deformities on display. But since they are merely animals, they have always been a secondary attraction: A sideshow to the sideshow. A few, such as the legendary Feejee Mermaid, received top billing and special tours under the guise of expert showmen like P. T. Barnum. Most, however, appeared in dusty, crowded collections of the bizarre and exotic known as dime museums (since the original admission fee was a dime). One of the most famous of these was Robert Ripley's *Believe It or Not*. Other animal freaks served as teasers that enticed rubes to go behind the curtain and enter the exotic, erotic, hypnotic world of the sideshow.

Classic animal freaks fall into three categories: Live animals, taxidermied animals, and "pickled punks"—dead animals preserved in jars of formaldehyde. The live acts are often little more than petting zoos with a few genetic anomalies, such as two-headed turtles and snakes. Most display exotic imported breeds, like Shetland ponies, which are native to a series of islands north of Scotland and are the world's smallest horses. Folks who had never left the local corn patch were amazed by these tiny creatures (which are about half the size of ordinary horses), but with the proliferation of photographs, television, and world travel, the allure of this and similar acts lies mostly in the past.

Pickled punks are almost always fetuses and babies that died at birth. In nature, two-headed beasts and animals with gross deformities rarely live longer than a few minutes, if they are born alive at all, which makes them perfect for pickling and displaying but useless for anything else. Pickled punks are often grotesque, but they are rarely gaffed.

Taxidermy is another story. Unlike the other two acts, taxidermied freaks are almost always gaffs. Why wait for a real two-headed sheep, when you can create one by simply sewing an extra head onto a dead sheep? With an occasional exception, the world of carnival taxidermy is a trick created to fool the eye into believing the impossible—or at least the highly improbable.

What these acts lack in honesty they make up for in originality and charm. The basilisk, one of the world's most famous gaffs, is the top of a rooster attached to the bottom of a lizard. The jackalope is a rabbit with antelope antlers sewn onto its head. The alligator man is the tail of a 7-foot or larger alligator hooked beneath the top half of a human skeleton. Thousands of people paid money to see the famous furry trout, the most common gaff of the nineteenth century, which is nothing more than a fish wrapped in an animal pelt.

The most famous animal gaff of all time is Barnum's Feejee Mermaid (he chose not to spell it Fiji). The "mermaid," which was about 3 feet long and displayed in a leaded glass box, was said to have been caught off a South Pacific island. In fact, it was the head of a monkey sewn onto the body of a giant fish.

Feejee Mermaid:
The girl of your dreams

The Feejee Mermaid became world famous and brought in millions of dollars due to two important factors. The first is ignorance. Few Europeans in the late 1800s had heard of the island of Fiji, so Victorians (who had never seen television or even color photographs) were willing to believe just about anything was possible there.

The second is morbid curiosity. The Feejee Mermaid was bizarre, hideous, and unlike anything most people ever expected to see. It was therefore worth the price of admission, generally a quarter, even if you didn't come away believing it was a real animal.

And therein lies the secret of the fake-animal freak tent: Price. An animal gaff doesn't necessarily have to be realistic, but it must always be priced low enough to keep the disappointed customer from complaining. If you want to pay for an animal freak show, always make sure the price conforms to this rule. Keep expectations low. Realize ahead of time that you are paying for showmanship, and enjoy the skill of the taxidermy, the brilliance of the staging, or the courage of the shameless proprietor.

If you want to make your own animal freak gaff, *always* use animals that are already dead. Discuss any plans with a licensed taxidermist *before* you begin, and make sure they teach you how to prepare and preserve dead animal flesh correctly. And remember that in the normal world it is not socially acceptable to play with dead animal parts. In fact, it is widely considered deranged. If you are discovered with a half-rotten squirrel head attached to the rancid tail of a giant carp, arguing that it's a mermaid won't keep you out of years of intense psychiatric therapy.

# Make it at home:
## Shrunken Head

Shrunken heads are a sideshow classic. A few were bought (or stolen) from the Jivaro tribes of the Amazon basin, who shrunk the heads of vanquished male foes. Many, however, were fakes you can easily re-create at home. The classic gaff uses a fresh apple. It takes a true artist to actually make an apple look like a real head, but it's fun to try nonetheless.

1. Choose the largest, freshest apple you can find. Peel it carefully, leaving only a little rind at the top and bottom.

2. Carve facial features into the apple. Make them bigger than real features because shrinkage will occur. Use toothpicks for the details and try not to cut too deeply, as gouges will show later on. When done, smooth and dry the surface of the "head" with a paper towel.

3. Immerse the apple completely in a solution of 1/2 cup salt, 6 cups water, and the juice of half a lemon. Soak for 24 to 48 hours, by which time the apple will be pickled and shrunken.

4. Jab a straightened paper clip through the apple core, bending it into a hook. Use this hook to hang the apple in a dry place for 2 to 3 weeks, during which time it will shrink and harden. The area must be dry or the apple will rot instead of shrink. Check regularly, as a rotten apple is pretty foul.

5. For a gruesome look, add a spot of charcoal to the hardened apple head and smudge it over the face with your thumb. Use black wool to sew the mouth shut. Real shrunken heads have very long hair, since hair doesn't shrink. Keep that in mind while decorating your shriveled monstrosity.

# The Talker

The key to the freak show, like all shows, is attracting customers. The key to attracting customers isn't colorful sideshow art, catchy as it may be; it's the outside talker. The outside talker is the person whose job it is to bring in the crowds.

Do not call the talker a barker. They do not like that term. As any talker will tell you, they are not barking at random passersby; they are performing an intricate, highly skilled talking act designed to whet the appetite of the discerning individual. They are doing this outside, in front of the show. Thus: *Outside talker.*

There are two types of outside talker routines: The grind and the bally. The grind is a talking pitch aimed at passing customers that touts the wonders hidden behind the curtain and the amazing feats performed live—right before your very eyes, ladies and gentlemen, boys and girls. Effective, yes, but only to the uninitiated.

The big money is made off the bally. The bally is a mini-show designed to draw a crowd. For the bally, the outside talker is joined by two or three of the "live" performers from the show. For some reason, sideshows always pitch the fact that their artists are currently alive. (The actual reason is to differentiate these acts from the other oddities covered by the admission price, such as wax figures and pickled punks.)

The artists do not perform their acts for the bally; they are the bait. It's the talker who works the crowd with a heated spiel, drawing spectators in with a few card tricks or illusions. Once the crowd is at a fever pitch, the talker "convinces" the owner or ticket-taker to offer a discount to the show—but only for the next two minutes.

The result is often a bunch of people staring slack-jawed at one another. After all, it's a freak show in there: Who really want to be the first to go inside? Suddenly, a person pulls out his money and rushes wide-eyed to the counter to buy a ticket, bumping a few shoulders along the way.

A feeble-minded stranger seduced by the dark side? Hardly. That wonder-blinded customer is a shill: An employee planted by the show to break the ice. A well-placed shill is the key to "turning the tip," the sideshow term for transforming sidewalk gawkers into a paying crowd.

A typical bally lasts 3 to 5 minutes and is performed before the start of each show (called a rotation). The frequency of the rotation depends on the type of show, the company, and especially the crowd. If there's a lot of foot traffic—on a Sunday weekend in July, for instance—the performers will squeeze in as many rotations as possible. On a dreary October day without many prospective customers, they'll take it easy and throw in a few special tricks or added features.

These days, the bally talker and the grind talker are almost always the same person, and the position can easily involve ten hours of continuous chatter. In the heyday of the carnival, though, the bally talker was an honored position: He wasn't expected to perform any other duties. Many bally talkers went on to become owners and operators. After all, they clearly had a knack for separating a sucker from his cash.

# From Fakirs to Entertainers

Make no mistake, sideshow performers are diligent and serious professionals who have spent years mastering their admittedly arcane skills. Popular acts like Human Blockhead (nail in the nose), fire breathing, sword swallowing, and glass eating are precise, death-defying stunts. Lesser acts like the electric chair, snake handling, insect eating, and the bed of nails may not involve intricate skills, but they do involve fearlessness and the mental discipline to endure pain—or eat grotesque food.

All these acts have a long tradition in America going back to the 1800s, but their true origins go back even further, to the Indian fakirs, a class of magicians and holy men that gained popularity as early as 1200.

The fakirs, as the English spelling of their name suggests, created some classic fakes. In rod-into-serpent, the "rod" is a snake immobilized with a finger to the back of the head and straightened into a stiff, sticklike shape. When the snake is thrown to the ground, it immediately regains its power of movement and slithers away.

Reaching a bare hand into a boiling pot of oil is also a fake. Unbeknownst to the spectators, the fakir adds a few cups of lime juice to the oil before turning up the heat. The lime juice boils at a very low temperature, and soon gives off crackling bubbles that make it appear the oil is scorching hot. In fact, the oil is barely above room temperature. The fakir plunges in his hand—and miraculously pulls it out of the "boiling" oil unscathed. A neat trick ... if you know exactly how long it takes your oil to boil. If your timing is off even thirty seconds, you can receive serious third degree burns on your hand, so please: This trick is for the experts only!

These fakes are exceptions to the rule. For the most part, the Indian fakirs created legitimate tricks. Instead of sleight of hand, they used extraordinary muscle control and discipline to perform seemingly impossible acts, a tradition that survives to the present day.

Remember, there are no fake acts in the modern freak show. Do not make an idiot out of yourself trying to "prove" that the stunt never happened. Don't poke, prod, or mock sideshow performers. They are literally risking their lives for your amusement. What more can you ask of another human being?

They are also entertainers, and mastering a death-defying talent is only part of the job. The key to an act isn't the stunt, it's the energy and charisma of the presentation.

Or, as magician Al Flosso once advised a sideshow wannabe: "Learn to be a showman, then learn some tricks."

# Melvin Burkhart:
# King of the Freaks

Sideshow artists are a tight-knit group. They respect their history. And if you poke around the circuit long enough, you'll hear one name again and again: Melvin Burkhart. Why? Because Melvin Burkhart was probably the greatest sideshow performer of the twentieth century.

Burkhart was a born showman and talker. With his trademark fancy fez and extraordinary range of tricks, he had the ability to command the attention of any audience. He was so versatile that, in the classic 10-in-1 traveling freak shows, Burkhart often performed six or seven of the acts. Sometimes, the only acts he didn't perform were the fat man and the midget.

Burkhart was a genuinely nice guy who took less talented performers under his wing and helped spread the fame (and profit) of the sideshow. Which is nice, but not superstar material. In the end, it was Burkhart's genius for innovation that made him a legend.

Melvin Burkhart was born in Louisville, Kentucky, in 1905. He was a class clown and natural performer, but singularly without talent . . . or so it seemed. Burkhart couldn't sing, dance, act, or tell jokes, but he could do one thing very well: Contort his body.

Soon Burkhart was performing his body contortions with a local vaudeville troop as an act called Anatomical Blunders. Contortion and escape had been popular even before the great Houdini, but Burkhart made his mark by turning his body into the centerpiece of the act. He would pop out his shoulder blades, jutting them back and forth. He would stretch out his neck like a rubber man. He would contort his face so that he smiled on one side and frowned on the other. And he would suck in his gut until his spine showed from the front, an act later billed as "The Human Skeleton."

Burkhart's Anatomical Blunders act became so popular that other performers started to copy it. Many came to Burkhart for training. Soon contortionists, once a novelty, were a mainstay of the Midway.

Enough for one lifetime? Hardly. This legend had an even bigger surprise hidden up his . . . nose.

While winning acclaim as the Anatomical Blunderer, Burkhart was also winning infamy as a terrible professional boxer. After six pro fights, all losses, his face was little more than a mass of broken bones. When Burkhart finally quit boxing, the doctors put him on the operating table and pulled a pile of bone fragments out of his nose with a long scalpel and pincer.

And that gave Melvin Burkhart an idea. The Indian fakirs had performed an act in which a sharp object was driven up the nose in order to terrify a skeptical audience. Burkhart realized that with his empty proboscis and nose for publicity he could transform that old torture stunt into a one-of-a-kind moneymaker.

But it wasn't just the act of pounding something into his head that made Melvin Burkhart's act unique, it was his ability to make that pounding into a crowd-pleaser. He added humor with a series of corny jokes, and he began to pound everything from railroad spikes to ice picks to cigars up his infamous nostrils. The humorous act was a major hit with families and children, and soon spread to every sideshow in the country. And thus a classic of the Midway was born: Human Blockhead.

Burkhart performed in sideshows for sixty-five years, most of them as a Human Blockhead. He is still the unofficial world record holder for largest-spike-driven-into-a-nose, having more than once used a spike the width of a pickle. He retired from Coney Island's Sideshows by the Seashore, the last stop on a long tour of the country's great sideshows, in 1985.

Despite his penchant for self-mutilation and misadventure, Melvin Burkhart lived a long and very full life. He died on November 8, 2001, at the age of ninety-four, only days after performing his Human Blockhead trick for the last time.

# Human Blockhead

Human Blockhead involves driving a nail or other object up your nose. Most people assume the act is a fake, but it's not. The nails are real, and they have not been dulled. The performer is actually hammering that sharp piece of metal into his head.

The effect is dramatic, but the concept behind Blockhead is actually fairly simple. All it takes is knowledge, concentration, and muscle control—something you can only learn in the sideshow, so don't try this at home.

The secret is that the performer drives the nail straight back into his nasal cavity, just above the mouth, and not up into the sinus cavity between his eyes. The same principle is involved in Mental Floss, which involves running a piece of cloth, a balloon, a chain, or even a condom (never dental floss, which will cut open the inside of the head) through the nose and out the mouth. A proper Blockhead shot can just barely be felt inside the roof of the mouth.

The key to Blockhead is knowing the limit, since driving too deep will cause serious bodily damage. Most performers pound the nail in about three inches, but the excruciating pain of bumping the back of the nasal cavity is the only sure sign the nail has hit the proverbial flesh wall—a wall, by the way, which is less than three-eighths of an inch thick, and the only thing between the nail and the base of the brain. That's why only pros should attempt this trick.

From a dramatic standpoint—and Blockhead is all about drama—the most important variable is the object being pounded. Most performers use ordinary hardware store nails. The sharpness of the point doesn't matter—the point isn't supposed to touch anything anyway—but the sides must be smooth. Even a small barb or nick can and will tear the delicate nostril lining to ribbons.

Most professionals use a nail that is exactly as deep as their head hole. Once the nail head is level with their nostril, they know they've reached their limit. This is not only safer than guessing, it's more dramatic. By the time they stop banging, the nail has all but disappeared.

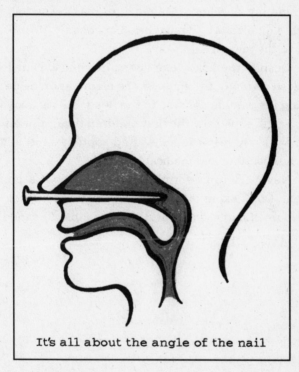

It's all about the angle of the nail

The key to Blockhead is playing up the fact that any slip, any error in calculation, is an instant lobotomy (and really, what can be worse than a self-inflicted lobotomy with a snot-covered nail?). Some performers use a small hammer to make the nail look bigger and more dangerous. Others use a large hammer to highlight the force of the pounding. Sideshow legend Todd Robbins uses the shoe off his foot. In all cases, the secret is the sound: A loud hammering is essential for full effect. That's why using a live microphone to beat the nail in is particularly impressive.

Another dramatic touch is the wince, usually when the second nail (in the second nostril) is halfway home, accompanied by a snappy one-liner. Melvin Burkhart coined the classic: "Ouch! I hit a bone . . . I must be a bonehead!" Most Blockheads defer to the master.

Despite the hokey one-liners, Blockhead is no joke. Even practiced correctly, the act tears the membranes inside the nose, causing irreparable damage to the head. This is uncomfortable and painful, especially the first hundred times. For an amateur, the most likely result is a deviated septum—and a lifetime of pain, humiliation, and medical bills.

Never try to perform Blockhead without a professional present. Don't experiment, because mistakes happen. You can hurt yourself badly, and regret that rash, blockheaded decision for the rest of your life.

# Sword Swallowing

The art of sword swallowing is more than four thousand years old, and is known to have been popular in the ancient cultures of India (where it originated), China, Japan, the Middle East, and Europe. The first sword swallower in America was an Indian named Sena Sama, who began appearing in 1817. It wasn't until the act's breakout success at the 1893 Chicago World's Fair, however, that it became a staple of the American sideshow.

Contrary to the opinions of loud-mouthed windbags, there is no illusion to this act. The entire sword is actually pushed down the throat and into the stomach. The danger is real. Only professionals, and those trained by professionals, should attempt this feat.

The equipment, of course, is of the utmost importance. The sword will be poking around more than two feet inside the body, so the edges must be so dull that they don't slice on contact. The point is rounded into a circle arc. The biggest danger of sword swallowing is sticking the sword too far into the body and touching the bottom of the stomach. With a rounded point, this is nauseating and painful; with a true tip, it can be fatal.

In addition, the blade must be nickel-plated, since chrome plating is more likely to flake off inside the digestive track. It must be impossible to separate from the handle, since there's nothing worse than pulling out the hilt and leaving the steel behind. And finally, the blade must be absolutely smooth, without any nicks, filigree, or etching, so that it doesn't snag on the esophagus or get caught on the stomach muscle.

As a rule, sword swallowing is a profession for neatniks. The sword must be cleaned after each insertion or stomach acid will corrode the blade. On off days, the sword must be stored properly to avoid deadly scratches or rust. The blade must be wiped down immediately before use. Even something as small as a hair or bit of dust can cause a gag reflex, and a serious injury.

The gag reflex is the sword swallower's primary enemy, which makes sense because it is the body's way of preventing you from doing something deadly and stupid . . . like swallowing

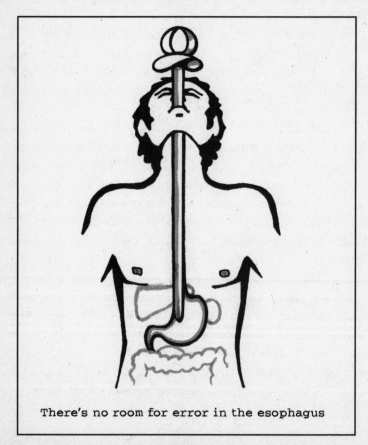

There's no room for error in the esophagus

a sword. If an object pushes its way into the esophagus without being chewed, the gag reflex kicks in and closes the throat muscles. This can't be prevented (it's one of the things that has kept our species alive, after all), but it can be dulled with repeated abuse. Professional sword swallowers tame the gag reflex with the finger-down-the-throat technique of the classic bulimic and work up to stuffing whole bananas and cucumbers into their mouths like third-rate porno actors.

With the gag reflex dulled, the sword can be slid slowly down the esophagus until it hits the stomach. The sword must then be forced past the muscle that closes the stomach. This causes that slight pause in the act—and results in terrible fits of vomiting for beginners.

Vomiting, however, is the least of the professional's worries. This act has killed—and killed publicly—many times. In fact, one of the world's great sword swallowers recently suffered multiple slice wounds to the stomach and esophagus during her act. She lost over a quart of blood and was extremely lucky to survive. Recovery took more than six months in the hospital.

The cause of the accident: A man from the audience tried to slip a $100 bill under her belt while the sword was in her stomach.

# Death by Swallowing

Sword swallowing is a deadly art that has killed many of its most ardent fans. Accidents happen, after all, especially when performers try to go from the extreme to the obscene. For instance, in 1970 a performer choked to death in front of an audience while trying to swallow a world-record thirteen swords at once. The incident prompted the *Guinness Book of World Records* to remove multiple-sword swallowing from its rankings, although the record was reinstated in the late 1990s.

By far the deadliest and most dangerous permutation of sword swallowing involves neon lightbulbs, which became part of the professional sword swallower's arsenal soon after their invention in the 1920s. As popularized by the mysterious "Prince Neon" in the 1930s, the act involves swallowing a standard 4-foot-long neon tube (the kind found in overhead lights at schools and offices) *while it's lit*, a real crowd-pleaser since the lit neon tube can be seen through the performer's neck.

Incredibly cool, yes, but also absurdly dangerous. First, in order to glow, the light must be plugged in. Obviously, it is never a good idea to stick live electrical equipment down your throat. Even worse, the thin glass tubes are extremely fragile. Even something as seemingly harmless as the difference in temperature between the tube and the throat can cause the light to crack. A slight bend in the esophagus, which is painful but correctable with a sword, will shatter the glass.

Once glass is broken off in the throat, emergency surgery is the only chance to save the performer's life. The esophagus is a smooth muscle, which means it contracts involuntarily when touched. This works great for food, but a shard of glass can become embedded in the muscle instead of sliding down into the stomach. The esophagus will continue to contract, trying to swallow the glass but instead shifting the shard around until it has sliced the throat to ribbons. This process will kill the victim in three to four days, an extremely gruesome and painful demise, which struck one of history's greatest sword swallowers (and first experimenters with neon glass tubes), England's Enno Strauss-Hanson.

# Glass Eating

Sword swallowing is dangerous: If you do something wrong, if you lose concentration, or if you're not in complete control, you'll wind up dead.

Glass eating is worse, because it can kill even when the performer does everything right. Consuming glass is an ancient form of torture practiced the world over. The Romans loved to execute prisoners by hiding glass shards in their mushy meals. And yet throughout recorded history many have embraced this masochistic exercise as a means of entertaining an audience... and putting bread on the table.

There is nothing positive about eating glass. It is indigestible, sharp, and totally without nutritional value. Even in the best (in other words, least deadly) of circumstances, painful mouth cuts are unavoidable. As few as two wineglasses a week can wear out the teeth completely in a few years. And eating is only a small part of the problem. The most dangerous moment of all comes about 48 hours after the act, when the undigested glass is passed out the other end. At any time between the entry and the exit, a cut can result in a hemorrhage or deadly internal bleeding. Perhaps that's why there are fewer than ten professional glass eaters in the United States today.

Most of these glass epicures prefer to dine on a standard lightbulb (although consuming wineglasses is also common). There are two reasons for this: First, lightbulb glass is very thin, which makes it easier to eat. Second, the performer can plug in the lightbulb and prove to any annoying skeptics in the audience that the glass is real. The bulb is then crushed and eaten. It is never bitten into whole, especially when lit. That's not an act—that's suicide.

# Breathing Fire

Breathing fire is the most popular of the ancient fakir arts. It has been the primary act of the wandering street performer since Europe's Middle Ages, when its practitioners were often tried as witches, and is still prominently featured in everything from heavy metal concerts to Las Vegas reviews. It's butch enough to impress even the brawniest gang member, and widely considered the sideshow act most likely to impress women.

But fire breathing is also profoundly dangerous. As the professionals like to put it, there are only two types of fire breathers: Those who've been burned and those who are going to be burned. If you don't know what you're doing, that first burn can be fatal. Never breathe fire without professional supervision. And never, never attempt the act with gasoline. Huffing off the local gas pump won't create a fireball, but it will make you sick, stinky, and brain-damaged.

The right fuel is one of the three keys to the perfect fireball, and it's the primary factor in the safety (or danger) inherent in the act. Using the wrong fuel (like gasoline) is the cause of most serious fire-related accidents. The type of fuel also has a direct effect on flame size, flame color, the explosiveness of the combustion (known as the flash point), and the amount of smoke. Professional fire breathers use a personal fuel mix, developed through years of experimentation, that gives them the ideal effect with a minimum of danger. Don't even bother asking for the formula, because they'll never tell you. After all, they've sweated through a lot of bad burns to find that perfect cocktail. Since you don't know the formula, don't try the act. It's that simple.

The second key to fire breathing is the vapor cloud, which determines the size and shape of the resulting fireball. A vapor cloud is created by filling the mouth with fuel, pursing the lips like you're going to kiss a frog, and forcibly blowing out. The amount of fuel in the mouth is unimportant; it's the ability to turn all that fuel into vapor that makes great fire. Professional fire breathers are masters of the form and can minutely control the placement, size, and shape of their vapor clouds. Watch closely and you'll notice a multitude of fire designs: Straight and thin (known as the dragon), mushroom, round with a puff of smoke, several short bursts, and giant ball.

Amateurs, meanwhile, often take a huge mouthful of gasoline or other hazardous sucker's fuel . . . and end up swallowing half of it or, even worse, breathing in while the fuel is in their mouth. That is one of the first things fire breathers learn: Never breathe in during the act because the fumes will

The giant ball is only one trick of the fire breather's art

scar the lungs. And never swallow. Spitting out is always better than throwing up.

The third and last key to fire breathing is the source of the flame. A fireball is formed when a spray of flammable liquid crosses paths with an open flame, so being able to control the ignition switch is vitally important. For this reason, most experts make their own torches. Kevlar is the wick of choice, crowning a wooden or plastic handle that won't heat up no matter how long the act lasts and the torch burns.

The fireball impresses, there's no doubt of that, but beyond the real possibility of death or serious facial scars there are other downsides to breathing fire. Fire-fuel smells terrible, and the inevitable spills on clothing stink for months. Singed facial hair is unattractive. Fire breath is nasty. And then there are the burps, which occur a few hours after ignition when the tiny amounts of fuel accidentally swallowed warm up in the stomach. These burps are perfectly healthy, but socially awkward. A small price to pay, perhaps, for the sake of art—but it just might cost you that cute girl who was so impressed with your act just a few hours earlier.

# The Bed of Nails and Hot Coals

The bed of nails and the field of burning coals have for centuries been associated with spiritual purity. They are acts of faith, a sign that with heaven's blessing a man can do the seemingly impossible. In some Native American cultures, the firewalker has been thought to be chosen by the gods; in India, the man who lies on a bed of nails is sometimes considered holy. As we know now, these acts aren't the result of divine intervention; they're simple physics.

The reason it's possible to walk on hot coals is that both wood and human flesh are poor conductors. Hot coals burn at about 1200 degrees Fahrenheit with an impressive fiery glow, especially at dusk. But because the fire is on the inside of the coal and not the surface, the heat is not transferred to the walker's feet. In addition, the walker's feet make contact with the coals for only a few seconds—long enough to impress onlookers, but not long enough to roast.

Like most carnival acts, firewalking sounds simple. But also like most carnival acts, many things can go wrong—especially if you're not experienced or cautious. The bed of coals must be no longer than 12 feet or exposure will be too prolonged. The coals must be dry hardwood, and they must be burned until they have a heavy layer of ash on the outside. Even in a correctly set coal bed, feet with thin skin will burn. Serious burns can occur if a piece of coal sticks to the bottom of the foot—a random accident that occurs with surprising frequency even among initiates—so this act should never be attempted at home.

The bed of nails is another ancient physics trick. Why does sitting on one nail produce a painful impaling? Because all your weight is concentrated on one point. But when the weight of the body is distributed over a thousand points at the same time, as it is on the bed of nails, no one nail is holding enough weight to even puncture the skin. To work correctly, the bed of nails must have at least four nails per square inch (although experts often use fewer). It doesn't matter how long the nails are, but they must be within one millimeter of the same length so that all nails are being utilized at the same time.

Physics keeps the act from being deadly, but that doesn't mean the bed of nails isn't painful. The nails hurt, especially when the true sideshow artiste adds a few stunts to impress the audience. One classic example is for the performer, while lying on the bed of nails, to call a member of the audience up onstage to stand on her chest. If you don't think this is painful, imagine lying on the ground and having your father or husband stand on your sternum. Now imagine the same trick . . . while lying on a thousand sharp points.

Even more ingenious is the classic bed of nails finale, in which a cinder block is placed on the artiste's chest and smashed by an assistant with a sledgehammer. With each blow,

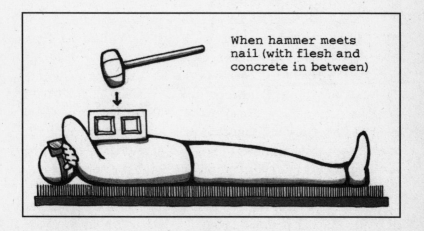

When hammer meets nail (with flesh and concrete in between)

the nails dig deeper into the performer's back, and the pulverized cinder block cuts deeper into the chest. And that's not to mention the flying concrete chips that force even the most foolhardy of freaks to don protective goggles. Of course, flying chips can put your eye out, but they don't make the act death-defying. Never fear, a deadly danger is present in the bed of nails: The sledgehammer. If the assistant follows through too enthusiastically, the direct blow can crush the chest cavity and stop the heart.

Again, imagine being hit full force in the chest with a sledgehammer. Now add a thousand very sharp spikes. Even a trick of physics won't save you from that bloody final finale.

# Beware the Flame...
# and the Booze

The sideshow is a tough life, and it has claimed more than a few victims in its day. Statistically, structural fires are the carnival's greatest killer, but more than a few sideshow artists have fallen prey to the very acts that put bread (and whiskey) on their table.

One common cause of mishap is ignorance. At the 1904 World's Fair, customers paid to enter a room and be bombarded with a massive dose of radiation. While it's neat to see your own bones, it's also dangerous, as proven a few years later by the death of radiation guru (and all-around great scientist) Marie Curie.

Sometimes, the incident is more hilarious than tragic, as in the case of a recent Electric Chair accident. In this classic act, the performer sits in an electrified chair that shoots out flames. One night, Coney Island artist Jason "Strange" Anderson had what seemed at the time to be a brilliant insight: If a little fire is good, more fire is better! In this deluded state of mind, he poured gasoline all over the chair, including the seat. Needless to say, during the act the flames flared out of control, forcing Mr. "Strange" to jump for his life. It was only then that he realized his gasoline-stained jeans were also on fire. He immediately dropped trou . . . only to discover that he wasn't wearing any underwear.

A similar, but more tragic accident occurred in the 1930s in Arizona. In a popular traveling act called High Dive, a woman would jump from a 50-foot platform into a 7-foot-deep tank of water. Her husband would then use gasoline to set himself on fire, back up to the end of the platform, and do two somersaults into the tank. The trick went over famously . . . until the couple fell to fighting and the man took to drink. One day, deeply intoxicated on the high dive, he poured too much gasoline on himself. As he struggled to bat out the flames, he slipped, fell 50 feet screaming and on fire . . . and missed the tank.

Excessive drinking also led to the untimely demise of sideshow legend Grady Stiles II. Like his father before him, Stiles was born with his hands and feet fused into "claws" and performed under the stage name Lobster Boy. Clearly this is a hard fate, and Stiles was soon driven to drinking— sometimes even onstage.

And then it all really fell apart. One night, during a drunken argument, Stiles shot his daughter's boyfriend to death from point-blank range (yes, Lobster Boy had several children). He was convicted of the crime, but fearing the famous freak would be harassed, beaten, and possibly even killed in prison, the judge let Stiles walk even though he ruled the crime was not self-defense. His generosity backfired, as Stiles's life spiraled further out of control. The lack of jail time made him feel invulnerable, and he became a violent wife-beater who terrorized his family for years.

In 1992, after decades of abuse, Lobster Boy was killed by a hitman hired by his wife and stepson, a Human Blockhead. And thus ended one of the most tragic and shocking lives in the American sideshow.

# Be a Freak

Perhaps the worst thing about being a sideshow freak . . . um, entertainer, is the constant barrage of questions.

**"How do you do it?"**

**"Is it fake?"**

**"What does it feel like?"**

**"Can you show me?"**

The answer to that last question is almost universally the same: No. The artist isn't going to show you how to swallow a sword just because you think it's neat. The Human Blockhead isn't going to do something stupid to "prove" the trick is real just because you're being an obnoxious jerk. The glass eater doesn't come down to the station and bug you about how you pump gas, right?

The secret to sideshow success is dedication. Learn your techniques, and learn your history. Know everything you can about performers before approaching them for advice. These people get a lot of yo-yos asking for a quick fix. If you can prove you're for real, you may just be rewarded with the technique or insider tip that will make you a star. But don't expect to be accepted overnight. A sideshow apprenticeship lasts two to three years, so be ready to put in long hours and suffer through countless nights of vomiting, cuts, and facial burns before graduating to the stage.

Even after you make it to the big time, you're not going to get rich fast. Top sideshow performers pull down about $500 for a 70-hour week—about the same wage as the fry cook at McDonald's. Average wages are about $350 a week. Some shows on the mud circuit, as sideshow artists call the traveling carnival route, pay little more than expenses.

The hot money is made at parties, corporate events, club shows, rock concerts, and yes, even bar mitzvahs. A private sideshow act can easily top $500 for a two-hour performance, and the only hassle is having to entertain a bunch of obnoxious children or drunken executives trying to make the moves on their secretaries.

The money may not be great, and the danger may be real, but any desk jockey will admit the sideshow beats pushing paper on the daily excitement meter. And how cool is it to be one of only 63 professional sword swallowers in the world? Much cooler than being an insurance adjuster, that's for sure.

# 6

# So You Want to Be a Carny:
# The Life Revealed

Carnies have a reputation as ex-cons, drug dealers, recovered (almost) alcoholics, and marginally homeless drifters. The stereotype is only partially true. While many carnies are missing teeth, most are honest, hardworking people just trying to give you a decent ride on the Tilt-a-Whirl.

# A Field Guide to Carnies

The carny world is complex.

OK, it's not that complex, but it does have its own caste system based on your job and time in the business. "Roughies" are temporary help hired to set up and take down the equipment. "Greenies" have just started traveling. "Troupers" are Greenies who have made it past their first year. If you're fully accepted into the carny community, you're a "Lifer." The only promotion from there is to become an Owner, which means buying a ride or cart. Most Lifers never save enough to become owners: If they wanted responsibility, they'd have gotten a job in the regular world.

What are you in the carny universe? Like all outsiders, you're a "clem."

Of course, different carnies have different personality traits: They are people, after all. So for all you clems and wannabes, here's a quick guide to the other side. For the sake of space and propriety, this list sticks with those carnies pumping testosterone. After all, it's a male-dominated world out there on the carnival lot.

# The New Kid

The New Kid is anyone who hasn't yet been accepted as a Lifer. He could be a college kid on a lark for the summer or a car thief on the run from the law. Doesn't matter, at the carnival they're all the same.

## Age:

18 - 25

## Hangout:

Second man on the rides; the worst job at the carnival.

## Dress:

Only carny wearing his company uniform (shirt only)

## Distinguishing characteristics:

Full head of hair

Nice wad of chawin' tobaccy

Quick eye for scoping lot lizards

## Hobby:

Sitting around thinking how nice it would be to have a girlfriend

## Clem Accessibility:

The New Kid is the only carny that hesitates before passing you off on someone else when you ask annoying questions. Don't pressure him: He's doing the best he can.

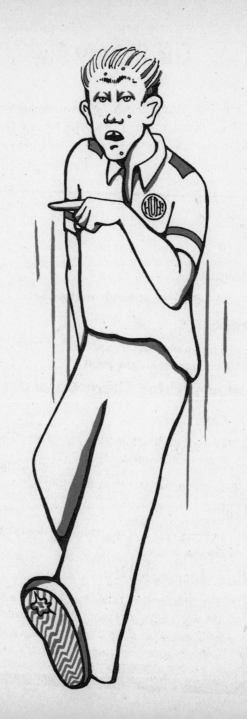

# The Skinny Guy

He may be skinny, but he's got muscles like ropes from dismantling all those 10-ton rides. The Skinny Guy is the only carny that looks like he's in shape—prison-yard shape, to be precise.

## Age:
22 - 35

## Hangout:
On-a-Stick food booth; dart games

## Dress:
Homemade muscle shirt paired with worn-out, skintight jeans

## Distinguishing Characteristics:
Facial scar

Tattoo on knuckles that says *Hate*, *Vera*, or *Ozzy* (not mandatory)

Less hair up top than he'd like

## Hobby:
Driving real fast, although he doesn't have a license or a car

## Clem Accessibility:
The Skinny Guy takes his job very seriously. He won't give you any freebies—ever—but he'll warm up a bit if you've got a good-looking honey on your arm.

# The Pro

The Pro has been around long enough to know that, whatever it is, it ain't no skin off his teeth. The Pro will look twice and shrug at a bent pole that's making the ride cars swing down toward the ground. He's seen it all before.

**Age:**

30 - 50

**Hangout:**

Ride operator; shooting games

**Dress:**

Jeans are too long and baggy, but shirt is working hard to stretch over his ample midsection

**Distinguishing Characteristics:**

Beer Belly

Feathery mustache and mullet

Fading tattoo from two-month stint in army as a teenager

Laid-back attitude

**Hobbies:**

Beer

**Clem Accessibility:**

Harmless, mostly because he couldn't care less about you.

# Mumbles

You get the feeling some people just don't fit in no matter where they are. At the carnival, that guy is Mumbles.

**Age:**

40 - 60

**Hangout:**

The ride operator booth; only comes out when absolutely necessary

**Dress:**

A shiny jacket from an auto supply store, even in 98-degree weather

**Distinguishing characteristics:**

Hat advertising farm equipment or other product from the life-not-lived

Square plastic-rim glasses too big for his face

Weak chin but surprisingly big ears

Poor shave

Doesn't look you in the eye

**Hobby:**

Hanging out in trailer planning new life and/or revenge

**Clem Accessibility:**

Don't even bother asking him a question— he didn't get his nickname for nothing.

# The Old-Timer

The Old-Timer is the king of the carnival and as cool (and scaly) as a crocodile. You'll find him talking up the clems at the hottest games, where the real money is made.

**Age:**

55+

**Hangout:**

Ball-pitching games

**Dress:**

Apron with lots of pockets crammed full of money

**Distinguishing characteristics:**

Long gray ponytail

Leathery skin from years in the sun

Perpetually lit cigarette or cigar

Leather apron hung with screwdriver, wrench, hole punch, and a roll of gaffer's tape

**Hobbies:**

Running a carnival—it's a full-time gig

**Clem Accessibility:**

The Old-Timer would love to help you, but he's got a thousand customers to deal with and every freaking moron at the carnival needs him to solve their stupid little problem.

# The Retiree

Successful businesspeople (often couples) are sometimes drawn to the carnival in early retirement. Some travel like true carnies, others are 40-milers who stick close to home. These jovial sorts aren't in it for the hustle; they just love the game.

## Age:
50 – 60

## Hangout:
Low-risk carny game; food booth

## Dress:
Button-down or golf shirt, khaki pants, comfortable shoes

## Distinguishing characteristics:
Give you a vague uneasy feeling you can't explain, until you realize they remind you of your parents

## Hobbies:
Gin rummy, television, collecting souvenirs from every stop on the carnival tour

## Clem Accessibility:
They love to chat—but if you wanted to hang out with the 'rents you could have stayed home.

# Greenies

It's easy to get a job as a carny: There's always an opening on the lot. The carny life is a tough haul, but conventional wisdom says that if you make it past the first year, you're hooked for life. Unfortunately, most people don't make it past the first month.

Before you join up, try your hand at temporary help. Go to the fairgrounds two days before the fair is scheduled to begin. It takes a while to assemble all the rides, touch up the paint, and level everything out. The ride carnies—or "mechanical entertainment technicians" as they like to be called—can always use help with the heavy lifting. Just remember to follow a few simple rules:

- **Act like the idiot you are.** Never pretend to be a real carny when you're just temporary help. Everybody at the carnival knows each other, so you're not going to fool them into thinking you're a Lifer. Besides, you have no idea what you're doing out there. The best you can hope for is to remember the lingo. If someone yells for a greenie or a roughie, they're talking about you. If anyone asks, you're just "doing a spot."

- **Gamey = lamey.** Even as a greenie, try not to get stuck stocking the game booths with toys or lining up tin cans in the shooting booth. These jobs are easy, but they're looked down on by the hard-core carnies. The last thing you want is a reputation as a "gamey."

- **Obey the carny code.** Whenever you're on the lot, you must obey the carny code: It is perfectly fine to sucker clems, but never steal from a fellow carny.

If you miss the setup, you've got another chance to dip your toe in the carny pool: The breakdown. Carnival companies break down the equipment immediately after the close of the last day, working all night to pack up and hit the road by morning. A carny workday is 14 hours; breakdown on a typical ride takes 10 hours, plus loading and tie-down. That means on the last day of a fair the carny is working close to 30 hours straight, the last third lugging hundreds of pounds of steel and fiberglass. Needless to say, help is always welcome.

The best news? Carnivals always pay cash.

# Help Wanted to Travel: No Hard Habits

You're not a real carny until you travel. It's not a hard gig to find, but it can be a pretty hard life if you aren't prepared.

- **First things first.** Don't try to hide in the carnival if you're on the run from the law. Carnivals check outstanding warrants on a regular basis, and you will be caught. This is especially true of child molesters. There is no place for perverts in the modern carnival.

- **Always find out in advance where you will be working.** Will it be food, rides, or games? Ask about the breakdown procedure. Don't be surprised at three in the morning by a job taking down steel beams 50 feet in the air without a harness.

- **Always check with other carnies before signing on with a company.** Search out greenies and ask them how they are treated, if the paychecks come on time, and how the accommodations are. Don't expect a palace—but don't settle for an old cardboard box, either.

- **"No Hard Habits" means no hard drug use.** If hard habits aren't mentioned, does that mean hard drug use is permitted? Anecdotal evidence points to yes, although the practice is never recommended.

- **Find out the length of your outfit's season,** and whether you're expected to work during the winter.

In the North and Midwest, the carnival season lasts from March to October. Some carnivals take the rest of the year off. Others travel to Florida or Texas where the carnival season lasts all year long.

Typical carny pay is about $200 a week after living expenses. Some companies pay a flat $200; others pay more, then deduct expenses. Always find out what you're getting and what you're keeping. It takes a little math, but it's worth the effort.

While rooms are always available, meals are only provided in the off-season, when pay can drop to as little as $50 a week. Since a carny is expected to work a 14-hour day, six or seven days a week in the high season, there is almost never a chance to eat off the fairgrounds. Meals are available for a reasonable fee in the cookhouse, a carnies-only establishment that usually consists of a bunch of long tables shoved under a tent. The other option is overpriced carny food, but even corn dogs and funnel cakes begin to look mighty unappetizing after eating them for a month straight.

Then there are the lot lizards: Locals attracted to the danger and anonymity of a carny sexual encounter. (Not to be confused with "lot lice," who are locals who just walk the grounds without playing the games or riding the rides.) Lot lizards aren't clean, and they don't hang around the next morning, but they are plentiful. Carny sex, at least with clems, is the very definition of casual.

And just like eating corn dogs every day, carny sex gets old. You don't believe it now, but spend a summer in the carnival and you will.

# Meet the Bossman

Don't worry too much about the company you hook up with for your first carny gig: They're pretty much all the same for a roughie. And since you're probably just walking on the lot and hitching on, you're not going to have a lot of choice. Check for the best option at that particular fair, sling your junk into the bunkhouse, and call it home.

Once you're on the road, you'll have a better idea what kind of company you're with. Most carnival companies are family-owned. All test for drugs and alcohol, but just like on any job some—OK, most—of the employees will be drug addicts or alcoholics. The living quarters will definitely be dreadful. That's just a fact of life for the roughie.

The biggest difference between companies is size. Major companies like Amusements of America (the "Big A") travel large territories, usually either the entire East Coast or West Coast. They have a long season—March 1 to December 1—and usually offer winter quarters or off-season gigs in Florida, Texas, or the Caribbean. No carnivals travel the whole country, so if you want to go coast to coast join the freaking circus. The carnival is a territorial business.

**The Big Leagues.** The Strates Company is a prime example of a big modern carnival operator. Founded in the 1920s by a carnival wrestler known as "Young Strangler Lewis," Strates was a mainstay of the southern carnival circuit during the Depression with an act that featured trained bears, a 37-inch-tall woman, and a star attraction called "The Monkey Motordrome."

Strates is still owned and operated by the Strangler's son. The company travels the eastern seaboard from Maine to Florida during its nine-month season, with an emphasis on rides and games, minus the freaks and monkeys.

The show employs close to 500 people, many of whom live on the company train. This sounds exotic—Strates is the last train carnival still operating in America—but the rooms are small and the beds are little more than a foam mattress on a piece of plywood. In other words, you're definitely working for the man.

**The Local Circuit.** The other option for would-be carnies is a small carnival operator. The typical small show travels to only three or four states, employs about fifty people, plays a lot of church picnics and county fairs, and closes up shop by the end of October. The close-to-home circuit can be a good gig, but close quarters can breed discontent. Your peace of mind, and peace of wallet, will depend on the carnival owner and your fellow carnies.

**The God Show.** Many carnival owners are Christian, with a mission statement about serving the Lord while giving little kids a good scare on the Tilt-a-Whirl. Don't be fooled. These owners mean well, but that doesn't mean they run a clean show. Carnies are tough to tame, and there are just as many druggies and alcoholics on the God circuit as there are with the big boys; they just tend to keep it a bit more quiet.

Once you ply the circuit for a few years, you'll figure out the system. While some companies retain the hard old ways of the carnival world, many now offer health insurance, and some even provide schooling for carny children. So don't settle: Go ahead and find a company that offers dental insurance. These days, chipped teeth don't have to be part of the show.

# Carny Quarters

Being a carny isn't just a job, it's a lifestyle. You're going to be on the road nine months a year, and you're not just going to be working in a carnival, you're going to be living in it.

The ultimate carny ride is the house trailer. Many house trailers are broken down retreads, fitted out by a carny family that has scraped together the money over several summers. These days, though, it's not unusual to see Winnebagos with DirecTV dishes parked on the back lot. Sometimes, it's good to be the bossman.

Other carnies opt for tents and do their own cooking on a charcoal grill. This can be a nice lifestyle when the weather cooperates, but it can get messy when it rains. Tents also offer little protection from those classic carnival pests: Flashing lights and blaring disco music.

Most carnies, especially roughies and troupers, live in the company-provided bunkhouse, called the LQ (for living quarters). The bunkhouse is usually a large fifth-wheel trailer that has been divided into several small (often 6 x 8 foot) rooms. A typical room contains two bunks and a dresser. Locks must be rented from the company. The shower and bathroom are in the center of the bunkhouse and shared by the eight to ten people living there.

Bunkhouses are co-ed, but rooms are strictly single-sex or serious couples only. If you bring a girlfriend or spouse, you can sometimes finagle a private trailer, or at least a private room in the bunkhouse, often referred to by carnies as a "honeymoon suite" (and not because of the Jacuzzi and beautiful view of the dew-dipped mountains in the moonlight).

If you're thinking of faking your way into the honeymoon suite, remember: You have to live with that woman, so think twice before acting like your sister is your girlfriend just to score a hot pad (unless she really is your sister *and* your girlfriend).

A bunkhouse room runs about $50 a week at most carnivals, paid either a week in advance or right out of the paycheck. Not a bad deal, really, unless you don't get along with your bunkmates. In the bunkhouse, there's not much shelter from a drunk, a screamer, or a roomy who loves the lot lizards.

All the comfort of prison, except you pay for the lock

# *Riding Solo*

It's one thing to be a company carny; it's another to hitch on to a carnival with your own trailer and amusements. This is definitely the way to live, if you don't mind a few lean years. As a greenie and an owner, you're going to get taken for a few rides. After all, the competition is a bunch of pros, and it takes time to build the personal relationships that are so important in the carnival trade.

There are three ways to go as an independent owner (or independent joiner as they're called in the carnival): Join a big company, join a small company, or hopscotch.

**The Big Boys.** A big company like Strates (see previous chapter) has its advantages: They plan your route, guarantee your spots, pay for your electricity and setup, and even cover your rent in a pinch. They will also end up owning you. As a greenie, you will get the worst spots on the lot. You will be sent to cover "blanks"—poor carnivals and fairs with few customers—and may end up losing your shirt. The company will give you a new shirt, but it will come at a very steep price.

**The Lonely Ride.** Hopscotching, or going independent, is where the money is. You set your own schedule, and you only play the dates you know will be profitable for your particular amusement. Unfortunately, as a newbie you have no idea where or when these moneymaking dates will occur, and nobody on the circuit is going to tell you. Sorry, but for the first few years, the big money's out of reach.

**The God Squad.** Your best bet as a newbie is the church fair circuit. Local companies will get you hooked up for a whole season in a three- or four-state region. It's not the most exciting circuit in the world, but you'll make a living and learn a lot about your attraction. You may find out it's not as cool (or as profitable) as you believe it is. Why do you think that old carny sold it to you in the first place?

The carnival season lasts from March to October, but you better cash in when the cash is flowing. Nice weekends in early spring, when the crowds are thick and ready to spend, are primo moneymakers. July Fourth weekend through the end of October is peak carnival season. You need to make enough money during this time to tide you over to the next spring. If not, it's going to be a long and lonely winter of canned beans.

No matter how desperate you are, don't go to Florida for the winter season. It's a zoo down there and the animals are fierce. Not to mix metaphors, but Florida is where the sharks come to circle the chum. If you don't know what you're doing, they will eat you alive.

The secret to success isn't working every show or persevering through a few lean years: Any sucker can die on his feet. The secret is learning from your mistakes, and taking the good with the bad. You'll hit blank dates that almost wipe you out. Don't get discouraged. You'll hit strikes where you're rolling in dough after a hot week. Don't get too excited, and whatever you do don't spend that cash, no matter how big your stash.

If you're in the carnival business, you're going to need the spare green some day very soon.

# Making Money on Snacks

Being a traveling food booth owner may seem like a glamour job, but it isn't easy. It's one of the dirtiest, hottest, and most difficult jobs on the Midway.

It also isn't cheap. The start-up fees for a cart and equipment can run from $15,000 to $50,000, depending on whether you want to go with new or used equipment. Then there are lot fees for your spot at the carnival site, which run at least $50 a square foot. That's not to mention the cost of electricity, travel, supplies, and labor.

Labor is expensive, both to pay and to keep on the road. A typical employee will snack away about 10 percent of your profits in the course of a day. Candy bars are especially tempting: More than 15 percent never make it to the sales counter, which is why you almost never see them sold by carnies.

The most successful carny cart team consists of two professionals: One to cook and one to sell. If preparing each item is too complex or if too many items are being sold, the formula doesn't work. That's why you never buy food from a mega-vendor or a gourmet traveler frying up salmon remoulade. These people are either inexperienced or cutting corners.

The good news is that most carny foods are cheap to produce. Nachos cost the vendor about 35 cents per serving; caramel apples cost 40 cents; sno-cones and funnel cakes 25 cents. Since all these items sell for between $1 and $3, the profit margin is high. Meat items can cost up to a dollar a serving, but since they can retail for up to $7 the profit is even greater with a grill than a fryer or an ice machine.

Still, given the high cost of labor and travel, a typical carny cart will make a profit of less than $40,000 for a ten-month year. Split that between two employees, factor in the high start-up cost, and nobody's getting rich.

But it sure beats working at Denny's.

# A Community of Carnies

Much has changed in the carnival in the last few decades. In many places, drugs are out and health insurance is in. Biological freaks are few and far between, at least as paid performers. The sideshow is dwindling and the gaffers are being run out by the honest folk.

The monthly publication *Billboard* (now known as *Amusement Business* or the *AB*) has been the bible of the carnival industry for more than fifty years, and old-time carnies read it religiously. In the 1950s, many carnies listed their address as a forwarding service at the *AB*. Now carnies use e-mail and the *AB*, though still published, is hard to find even on the carnival lot.

But one thing hasn't changed: The carnival is still a family, whether you're a freak, a sideshow artist, or a trouper. If you're in the carnival you're "with it," and the other carnies will spot you in a crowd of clems. More important, a fellow carny will always cover your back. That's just another aspect of the carny code.

If you don't believe it, visit Gibsonton, Florida, the city that carnies built. Gibtown, as it's known, has grown from the original winter home of Ringling Brothers circus to a modest city of 7,000 people. Most of the people live in trailers or ordinary ranch homes, and those who work there have perfectly ordinary jobs. What makes the city special is that most of the residents are retired freaks, circus performers, and carnies.

Gibsonton is probably the only town to have a giant as the police chief and a midget as the fire chief at the same time, which occurred in the 1940s. It was the retirement home of deceased sideshow stars like Sealo, Lobster Boy, and Melvin Burkhart. Jeanie "The Half Girl" ran the bait-and-tackle shop for decades. Elephants have been spotted roaming the streets, and Gibtown undoubtedly has more clowns per square foot than any other city in the world. And, just to show government can be thoughtful, the post office even has a lower table so the dwarves can sort their mail in comfort.

But times are changing in Gibsonton, just as they are in the rest of the carnival world. The current residents are mostly retired carnival owners and ride operators, instead of freaks and sideshow artists. These carnies are born showmen and performers, but more and more they are starting to look and act like the rest of America.

Still, in a world of strip malls, chain restaurants, and big box stores, Gibtown offers a refreshing change from the every day. It's got energy; it's got excitement; it's got oddness and attitude and a little danger.

In other words, Gibsonton's got the spirit of the carnival, and once you've got the carnival under your skin you can never, ever wash it away.

# Sources and Acknowledgments

This book is based on the knowledge and
experience of hundreds of people who know
more than I do. I am eternally grateful to the
countless nameless carnies who taught me (and
often schooled me) via their actions,
inactions, and advice.

I would especially like to thank the Amazin' Blazin'
Tyler Fyre of Coney Island's Sideshows by the
Seashore; Gold Medal Fun Products Company
(**www.gmpopcorn.com**), whose catalog of carny
equipment and food products gave me hours of
pleasure; roller coaster freak Ian Marshall;
Matthew Gryczan for his fascinating book
*Carnival Secrets*; the California Fair Services
Authority, especially Safety Manager Thomas W.
Allen; and Tom Hoey and his extraordinary carny
billboard and website, **www.carnivalbiz.com**.

This book could not have been written
without my friend Ian Christe.

Amy Wilson's wonderful page designs never
failed to inspire me with confidence, even when
I missed my deadlines.

To all those who inspired and informed:
Todd Robbins; corn dog king Zelindo Viscusi; Danny
Gowler; **www.snopes.com**; Jennifer at Sideshows
by the Seashore; Johnny Fox at the Freakatorium;

the public relations departments at Magic Mountain,
Disney, Cedar Point, Playland, and Kennywood; Wells
Tower; **www.backwashzine.com**; Brian Richardson;
**www.saferparks.org**; the Magic Café; the Disney
fanatics at **www.hiddenmickeys.org**;
Shoot the Freak-aholic Mark James; *Wall Street Journal*
reporter Brooks Barnes; ace researcher Betsy Davis;
pie-baking champion Judith Labiner; the roller coaster
statistics database at **www.rcdb.com**;
**www.themeparkinsider.com**; Strates Shows; the
Florida and Indiana fair inspection offices;
the documentary *Gibtown*; American Coaster
Enthusiasts; The Loop; the Consumer Product Safety
Commission; the highly recommended book *Freaks,
Frauds, and Fakirs*; and the dear departed
Melvin Burkhart, forever the king.

Bret Witter has been a carnival and amusement park enthusiast since his first visit to the North Alabama State Fair in 1978. A professional writer and editor, he lives in Queens, New York. This is his first book.